STUKELEY'S 'STONEHENGE'

Stukeley d.

Stukeley's 'Stonehenge'
An Unpublished Manuscript
1721–1724

Edited by
Aubrey Burl and Neil Mortimer

Yale University Press
New Haven and London

Designed by Sally Salvesen
Set in Monotype Baskerville by SNP Best-set Typesetter Ltd., Hong Kong
Printed in Britain by Cambridge Printing

Library of Congress Cataloging-in-Publication Data

Stukeley, William, 1687–1765.
Stukeley's 'Stonehenge': an unpublished manuscript, 1721–1724 /
[edited by] Aubrey Burl and Neil Mortimer.
p. cm.
Includes bibliographical references and index.
ISBN 0-300-09895-2 (cloth : alk. paper)
1. Stonehenge (England)--Early works to 1800. 2. Megalithic monuments--
England--Wiltshire--Early works to 1800. 3. Wiltshire (England)--Antiquities--
Early works to 1800. I. Burl, Aubrey. II. Mortimer, Neil. III. Title.
DA142.S895 2005
936.23´19--DC22

2005000821

FRONTISPIECE: *A Peep into the Santcum Sanctorum,*
6 June 1724, from *Stonehenge,* 1740
TITLE PAGE Portrait of Stukeley,
the frontispiece to *Stonehenge,* 1740

CONTENTS

ACKNOWLEDGEMENTS

The editors would like to record their gratitude to people who have been generous with information and advice.

Daniel Huws, former Keeper of Manuscripts at the Central Library of Cardiff and J. Brynmor Jones, Librarian in the Local Studies Department there were very helpful in their information about the source of Stukeley's Stonehenge manuscript, 4. 253, the subject of this book.

Mr D. W. Large, Church Archivist of St Mary Magdalene, East Ham, kindly sent information about that fine Norman church in whose cemetery William Stukeley is buried.

The constructive comments of the advisor for Yale clarified several uncertainties in the text. They have been resolved.

Russell Lawson solved a Roman problem. Quentin de la Bédoyère successfully traced the origins of the idolatrous custom of 'Markolis'.

Very special thanks must be given to Adrian James, assistant librarian of the Society of Antiquaries of London for volunteering to search the poorly-indexed pages of early volumes of the *Philosophical Transactions* for several of Stukeley's inexact references; and to Patricia Buckingham of the Bodleian Library for her attempt to locate another reference somewhere in the blackly inked-through lines of page after page in Stukeley's first manuscript about Celtic 'temples'.

The staff of Yale University Press were meticulous in their editing of a demanding text.

NOTE TO THE READER

In the text of the manuscript that follows three matters require explanation:

(1) *Measurements*
In his manuscript Stukeley expressed distances in the Imperial Units of miles, yards, feet and inches. He also used the ancient body-measurements of Cubits and Palms. Stukeley's 'Druid Cubit' of 20.8 inches (1 ft $8\frac{3}{4}$ ins) is 0.53 m. The Palm of $3\frac{1}{2}$ inches equals 8.9 cm.

In the transcription measurements exceeding 10 feet (3.05 m+) are followed by their metric equivalent. For shorter lengths the metric counterparts are:

Feet	Metres	Inches	Metres
1	0.31	1	0.024
2	0.61	2	0.049
3	0.91	3	0.076
4	1.22	4	0.101
5	1.52	5	0.128
6	1.83	6	0.152
7	2.13	7	0.177
8	2.44	8	0.204
9	2.74	9	0.229
10	3.05	10	0.253
		11	0.280
		12 = 1 Foot	

So that 9 feet 11 inches (9′11″) becomes 2.74 m + 0.28 m = 3.02 m.

(2) *Quotations*

In his need to find descriptions that might provide parallels for the customs of the unknown prehistoric societies that built and used Stonehenge Stukeley searched through the records of historical authors such as Homer and Virgil for accounts of burials, festivals and warfare. He frequently quoted from them, usually in the original Latin, occasionally in Greek, and frequently at length.

To help the reader only the first line of the original Latin or Greek is cited. It is followed in square brackets by a translation. Where known the source is given and so is the translator of the passage.

For two reasons this has not always been possible. Stukeley did not invariably name the author. When he did it was sometimes as a single, unreferenced line from a work like Virgil's *Aeneid*, an epic of twelve books and thousands of lines. Despite this lacuna considerable efforts have been made to locate and translate the quotation.

(3) *Miscellaneous papers*

The manuscript is accompanied by a handful of unnumbered loose sheets. Those sheets that relate to Stonehenge are transcribed in Appendix 1. Other sheets have nothing to do with Stonehenge. Rather than ignore these unrelated notes and pages, they have been listed in Appendix 2 at the end of the Stonehenge text.

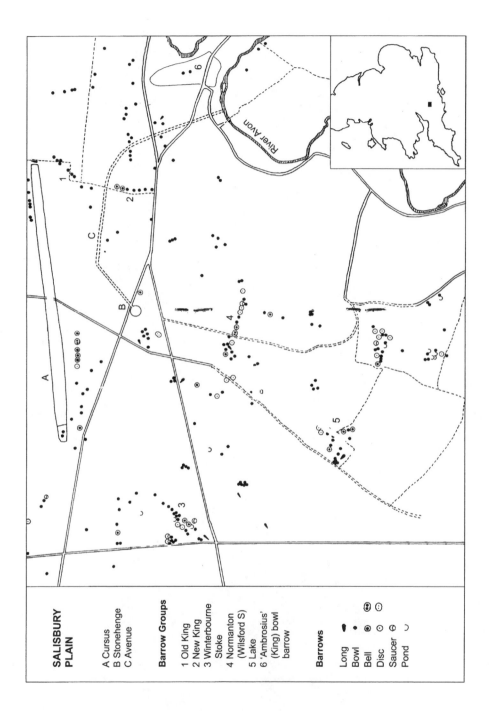

SALISBURY
PLAIN

A Cursus
B Stonehenge
C Avenue

Barrow Groups

1 Old King
2 New King
3 Winterbourne
  Stoke
4 Normanton
  (Wilsford S)
5 Lake
6 'Ambrosius'
  (King) bowl
  barrow

Barrows

Long
Bowl
Bell
Disc
Saucer
Pond

River Avon

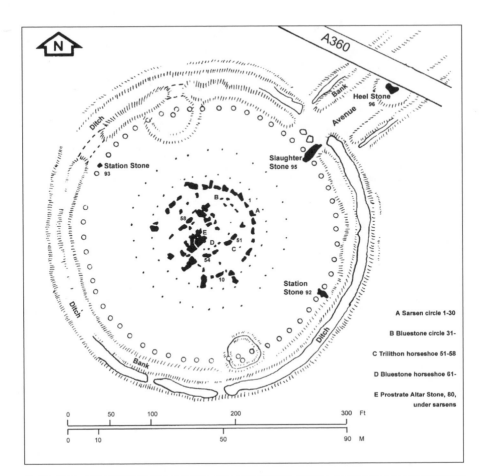

A360

N

Heel Stone 96

Bank

Avenue

Ditch

Slaughter Stone 95

Station Stone 93

B
58
E
D
51
C
54
10

Station Stone 92

Ditch

Ditch

Bank

A Sarsen circle 1-30

B Bluestone circle 31-

C Trilithon horseshoe 51-58

D Bluestone horseshoe 61-

E Prostrate Altar Stone, 80, under sarsens

| 0 | 50 | 100 | 200 | 300 | Ft |

| 0 | 10 | 50 | 90 | M |

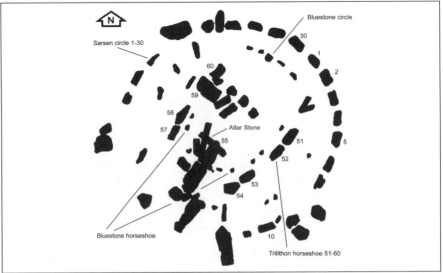

N

Bluestone circle

Sarsen circle 1-30

30
1
2
60
59
58
57
51
5
52
Altar Stone
55
53
54
10

Bluestone horseshoe

Trilithon horseshoe 51-60

Introduction

The History of the Manuscript

This is an annotated transcription of an early manuscript by William Stukeley about his early work at Stonehenge. It has remained unpublished, even in part, for well over two hundred years. It consists of some one hundred and forty pages varying in length from full pages to sheets of one or two lines.

In 1984 Professor Richard Atkinson, who had been informed of a Stonehenge manuscript in the Local Studies Department of Cardiff Public Library by Professor Stuart Piggott, kindly sent Aubrey Burl a photocopy of the Manuscript. It consisted of the fieldwork notes written by Stukeley during and just after his researches at Stonehenge in 1721–4, supplemented by thoughts added as late as April 1754. The inclusion of those additional pages reveals very clearly the unscholarly changes in Stukeley's thinking about druids, stone circles and religion after his decision to be ordained in the Church of England in 1726.

The manuscript is an important archaeological document for two reasons. It is very informative about early research at Stonehenge. It is also informative about the manner in which Stukeley's dispassionate interests in antiquity became tainted by an obsession that prehistoric Druids had been proto-Christians who introduced a pure religion into western Europe. The contrast between the sober contents of the manuscript and the unbalanced, unsustainable theories a decade and a half later in Stukeley's published *Stonehenge a Temple Restor'd to the British Druids* of 1740 is remarkable.

After Stukeley's death in 1765 his manuscripts were dispersed. There is a good list of the present location of most of them: the Bodleian Library, Oxford; Corpus Christi College, Cambridge; Freemasons' Hall, London; the Local Studies Department, Cardiff Public Library; the museum of the Wiltshire Archaeological Society, Devizes; the Royal College of Surgeons; the Royal Society, London; the Society of Antiquaries of London; the Wellcome Institute for the History of Science and Medicine.[1]

What happened to many of the papers between 1765 and the early nineteenth century is not always clear. In 1845 John Britton, topographer and antiquary, stated that he had owned letters from Stukeley to his colleagues, some miscellaneous writings and several other pieces 'for many years'. He would willingly have sold them for £60 but the British Museum refused the invaluable collection even for £50.[2] Britton died on 1 January 1847, and his library was sold. There was nothing of Stukeley's in the auction. The papers had gone to 'a descendant of the antiquary'.

Unknown to Britton the papers had been stolen before coming into his possession and shortly before his death they were reclaimed by their rightful owner, the Rev. Harris Fleming St John, of Kenwick Grange near Worcester, who eventually sold everything for £20.[3] Before that, however, St John had permitted the Rev. W. C. Lukis to edit Stukeley's considerable correspondence in three volumes.[4] Other manuscripts were in the private library of Mr. R. F. St Andrew St John of Ealing.[5]

The manuscript of Stukeley's notes about Stonehenge, MS 4.253, was once believed to have been purchased by Cardiff Public Library in 1896 at a sale of the library of Sir Thomas Phillipps, Middle Hall, Gloucestershire. More probably only one of the six items of Stukeley memorabilia at Cardiff, M. 4. 26, came from there and the 'Stonehenge' manuscript was bought at a later auction some time between 1920 and 1925.[6] MS 4.253 is an expanded version of Part II, the Stonehenge section, of a set of notes on Celtic religion entitled 'The History of the Temples of the Antient Celts', about prehistoric henges and stone circles. Part I, a more general review, is in the Bodleian Library, Oxford, MS Eng. Misc. c. 323.

Following his fieldwork at Avebury from 1719 to 1723 Stukeley wrote down his archaeological notes. Stuart Piggott thought the writing was finished in 1723. David Boyd Haycock considered the 'History' had taken longer up to 1724.[7] Piggott, who had been interested in Stukeley and the druids since 1935, believed that Stukeley 'began work in 1719 in a purely objective record', a project that involved a ruthless 'wholesale plundering' of the invaluable 'Templa Druidum' about stone circles in John Aubrey's unpublished 'Monumenta Britannica'. Stukeley also extracted information from Edward Lhuyd's unpublished field-notes. The debts were not always acknowledged. Piggott added that Stukeley's observations about Avebury and Stonehenge 'were of course entirely original fieldwork set out in objective detail'. In the Bodleian Library the present writer found that only at the very end of Part II, on the final page, did the Druids become a Celtic priesthood associated with megalithic monuments. They were not yet christianised.

Haycock considered Piggott to be mistaken about Stukeley's later conversion. Although being 'a respected prehistorian and archaeologist' Piggott was 'chary about drawing conclusions', stating that the matter of prehistoric ritual 'must remain unknown, thanks to the very nature of archaeological evidence'.

Haycock buttressed this by quoting the words of Hayman about Piggott's reticence: 'It reveals a caution-neurosis in archaeologists which even today has not been eradicated'. Unfortunately, Haycock omitted Hayman's very next sentence, 'For an archaeologist writing in 1959 this was a very proper, even admirable, thing to say'.[8] The present writer, having spent almost half a century researching the almost irrecoverable rites performed in prehistoric stone circles, would agree unreservedly – in 2005!

Ironically, historians might use the same caution with their 'more reliable' sources. Archaeological evidence is mute but unprejudiced. A broken pot has no intention to mislead whereas many historical chroniclers were propagandists rather than objective recorders of the past.

In this respect it was relevant for Haycock to quote Michael Hunter about John Aubrey's 'Monumenta Britannica': 'the origin and growth of archaeology depended on the realisation that such uninscribed antiquities, if collated and compared, could lead to conclusions not available from historical sources'. Hunter had already pointed out that 'modern archaeology differs from other historical disciplines in its use of non-literary, material relics like pot-sherds and earthworks to reconstruct the human past in contrast to the written records valued by the historian'.[9]

It is less confusing to struggle against the silence of a standing stone which has no lies to tell than to wriggle with the circular arguments of some mediaeval polemicist fluently omitting inconvenient facts. Archaeological material is inherently honest.

Stone circles have no thought of deception. Their ravaged remains on Machrie Moor in Arran are just that: ruined rings of inorganic stone without life, tongues or telepathy. If they have a message it is for the archaeological fieldworker on Arran to decipher it.

Quite different from the lifeless rings on Machrie Moor were the human fantasies of an extremely biased 'historian'. Sir Thomas More did have a message, and it was knowingly perverted. His *History of Richard III*, c. 1521, is full of hints, sly allusions and devious misinterpretations. As a 'history' it is risible. It is inaccurate, an embellished narrative, 'always concerned to portray Richard as a grand villain'. It was written by a very well-educated man 'and was (apparently) broadly accepted by [his] equally well educated peers'. Yet as Horace Walpole observed in 1768, Thomas More 'was an historian who is capable of employing truth only as cement in a fabric of fiction'.[10]

It is necessary to stress this essential difference between wordless archaeological evidence and the often selective sentences of historical records because Stukeley, from 1719 until about 1724, was thinking archaeologically. It was only a few years later that 'history' as it was understood in the early eighteenth century, coupled with a contemporary ferment between traditional and free-thinking Christianity, betrayed him and corrupted his initial thoughts about Stonehenge.

It remains unknown exactly when Stukeley decided to convert his Iron Age druids into the forerunners of a Christian priesthood. There is nothing in the present manuscript, nor in the two 'Antient Celts' manuscripts in the Bodleian except for the one terminal page, nor in Stukeley's extensive correspondence before 1729, to disprove Piggott's contention. Nor is there anything to support Haycock's conjecture. The question was discussed at some length in *Avebury Reconsidered* by Peter Ucko and colleagues.[11] In the absence of any clarifying evidence the question must be left unresolved.

There were faults in the manuscript. The picture of ancient Britain was inevitably more hopeful than historic. Almost nothing was known about those pre-Roman centuries, but if the prehistory was poor the archaeology was not. It was clear and detailed. Its insights make its long-delayed publication all the more important both to the archaeologist and to the historian.

Stukeley suffered from two considerable handicaps, one, his arithmatic, perhaps wilfully inflicted. The other was an ignorance of pre-Roman Britain before about 80 BC. In his *Gallic Wars* Caesar mentioned the Belgic king, Diviacius, who had held part of Britain for a decade or so before 57 BC. Before that there was no history. Caesar could only add that it was thought that Druidism had started in Britain, adding 'and today those who would study the subject more accurately journey, as a rule, to Britain to learn it'.[12]

Sixty years before Stukeley, the perceptive John Aubrey had realised that stone circles could be found in parts of Britain where the Romans, Saxons and Danes had never been. Yet the rings were obviously 'of the same fashion, and antique rudenesse; wherfore I Conclude, that they were Works erected by the Britons: and were Temples of the Druids', going on to follow Caesar's statements that the cult had begun in Britain, that the Druids were priests and law-givers, not militant, had a long training, were knowledgeable about astronomy and believed in the immortality of the soul.[13]

In the total absence of contradictory facts it was understandable that Stukeley should accept the information. What was not understandable was his readiness to adapt his own mathematical calculations to agree with his ideas about a druidical unit of measurement. He may have been semi-numerate. More probably he was so convinced that the unit had existed that any lengths and distances that did not conform to it must be wrong.

As will be seen in the manuscript, he was confident that other surveyors had been careless in their measurements and contradicted Inigo Jones, Walter Charleton, John Aubrey, even John Wood the architect. If their calculations did not fit with his Druids' Cubit then they were wrong.

The mistaken prehistory and the corrupt arithmetic are faults in the manuscript and can be clarified. Where Stukeley's work excels, however, is in its clear-sighted, unprejudiced observations about what could physically be seen and explained at Stonehenge, even minutiae such as the slight curvature of the lintels, the relationship between the worked surfaces of the bluestone horseshoe and the unsmoothed pillars of the bluestone circle. These and other matters had never before been noticed. No one had bothered.

In his ledger Stukeley made his initial notes on the right-hand, recto, odd-numbered pages of his book. If he added to them later he did so on the left-hand, verso, even-numbered pages so that page 12 faced page 13 and was written on the back of page 11.

The handwriting on the rectos is neat, written in regular, closely spaced lines and gives the impression of a unitary composition. The versos are in a variety of hands, some similar to the recto, others less tidy, some almost sprawling, as might be expected if these were notes added over several years.

To help the modern reader the transcription of the manuscript clarifies this by interposing the additions between the original pages. This is shown by inserting page-numbers in square brackets above each section, for example page 5 begins with a continuation of Stukeley's page 3 followed by extracts from pages 4 and 5; this final section of page 5 continues on page 7.

References to notes are indicated by superscript numbers —[23] — within the text. They run consecutively throughout the pages and are listed in the Notes at the end.

Full stops have been included where Stukeley omitted them. To indicate this the first word of the next sentence does not begin with a capital letter.

The manuscript is an excellent account of Stukeley's dispassionate field-work at Stonehenge. It cites dimensions, converting them into an innovative Druid's Cubit. Stukeley discusses the design of the circles and 'horseshoes', describes the shaping of stones, announces his discovery of the avenue and the enigmatic cursus.

His comments are not limited to Stonehenge. He wrote about the surrounding long and round barrows and the excavation of some of them. The result is a splendid review of what could be said about the circle three centuries ago.

The manuscript is a fine example of Stukeley's clear thinking about antiquities before the 'Druidomania' of his later years.

William Stukeley (1687–1765)

In May 1719 when he first visited Stonehenge William Stukeley was a medical doctor who had moved to London from Boston, Lincolnshire. Still to become one of Britain's earliest archaeologists, he was at that time little more than a dilettante, delighting in superficialities of the ancient past and in curious events. Thunderstorms, Roman villas, eclipses, church architecture, folk stories, everything antique or unusual fascinated him. He had already enjoyed three long sight-seeing tours with friends but these were not research projects into prehistory.

Even on the latest tour in 1712 he had looked at Roman remains in Grantham, seen novel weaving-looms in Nottingham, noticed wild cherry-trees and rare plants, avoided tumbling into coal-pits and lead-mines in Derbyshire, crawled into a druid's grotto, was let down in a bucket to the bottom of a salt-quarry at Northwich, rode to Manchester and Lichfield, and had ended at Tamworth with comments about Aethelfleda, 'Lady of the Mercians', daughter of King Alfred, but had not mentioned one pre-historic site.[1]

This was in contradiction to his avowal that he had 'conceived great notions of the old Britons betimes, and longed to hear a language spoke soon after the deluge'. Despite this admirable aim he and his companions contrived to overlook every megalithic burial-place and stone circle in the Peak District and rode by the High Bridestones chambered tomb near Stafford without a word.

By 1719 Stukeley's interests were more focussed. The real mysteries of the remote past began to obsess him. Learning of the miscellanies about burial chambers and stone circles compiled by John Aubrey (1626–97) and Edward Lhuyd (1660–1709) he committed himself to the labour of copying their manuscripts whose descriptions, sketches and plans had no predecessors. Already, in 1716, he had written, 'Happening to fall into a Set of thoughts about Stonehenge in Wiltshire . . . I undertook to make an exact Model of that most noble and splendid piece of Antiquity'. He made one.

By copying from Aubrey and Lhuyd Stukeley preserved records of monuments either unlisted or vanished today. Intermingled with what he had transcribed from others were records of his own more studious travels between 1721 and 1725 after which he effectively gave up fieldwork. But he had made records.

Unsatisfied by his records, he interpolated observations among his copied notes in his 'Commonplace Book', now in Devizes Museum. Briggs showed that the description of a Roman bucket, purportedly seen on Stukeley's 'Itinerarium Cimbricum' of 1712, was actually included 'between 1720 and 1725 at a time when his interest in the systematic recording of archaeology was awakening'.[2]

There was other material. Friends like Roger Gale and colleagues such as William Borlase in Cornwall and Alexander Gordon in Scotland supplied him with information about little-known sites but the major authorities for the entries in the 'Commonplace Book' were John Aubrey and Edward Lhuyd, both of them deceased and their work unpublished.

In the late seventeenth century a friend of Aubrey's, Thomas Gale, Dean of York, made a draft of Aubrey's 'Monumenta Britannica', a manuscript compilation of letters, notes and jottings about ancient monuments that included a '*Templa Druidum*' section on stone circles. Roger Gale, who inherited his father's library, showed the copy to William Stukeley who retranscribed a great part of the manuscript onto the first thirty-eight pages of his 'Commonplace Book', ending 'Thus far Mr Gale's Notes out of Mr Aubrey's Collections 10 Dec 1718 W. S.'[3] Stukeley thus made a copy of a copy, the original sheets at that time being in the possession of Awnsham Churchill, a London bookseller.

On Aubrey's death in 1697 Churchill still had the unpublished manuscript. Between 1755 and 1780 it remained with a nephew of the same name. By 1817 it was owned by William Churchill, his son. Ultimately it passed to Colonel William Greville who finally sold the papers to the Bodleian Library, Oxford, in 1836. There they rested, almost in oblivion but secure, until their publication in two rather unsatisfactory volumes in 1980 and 1982.[4]

Stukeley therefore had access to unique information about a multitude of obscure sites from Land's End to the Orkneys and from eastern England to Ireland. He supplemented this archaeological treasure-house with further records of Welsh, Scottish and Irish antiquities assembled by the Welsh antiquary, Edward Lhuyd, who had made wide-ranging surveys in the late seventeenth century but whose collections also remained unpublished. A transcript of them was lent to Stukeley by another Fellow of the Society of Antiquaries, John Anstis. The news fascinated him and he determined to undertake his own fieldwork, examining in detail sites in southern England conveniently close to London, Stonehenge and Avebury.

It was exactly seventy years after Aubrey's recognition of Avebury that Stukeley went there in 1719, being intrigued by Aubrey's description of the earthwork enclosure and stone circles. He did not acknowledge his debt. On the contrary he claimed the discovery for himself. 'In 1718, Mr. Roger and Sam. Gale and I took a journey, through my eager desire, to view Abury, an antiquity altogether unknown'.[5] This was not only a lie. It was a preposterous lie. The year was wrong. The visit was in 1719 by which time Stukeley had already copied the 'Monumenta Britannica'. Aubrey's account of Avebury, moreover, had been published over twenty years earlier in the 1695 edition of Camden's *Britannia*, 111–12. It was ungracious to ignore such evidence.[6] The discourtesy would probably not have bothered Aubrey whose generosity and good humour made him a welcome guest to his wealthy friends and from whose country houses he made many of his fieldwork sorties.

The antiquarian travels of Stukeley in the Home Counties and the west and north of England between 1710 and 1725 were published in his *Itinerarium Curiosum, I, II*, enlarged in the second edition of 1776. They provide an explanatory background to Stukeley's work at Stonehenge itself between 1721 and 1724 when in the company of colleagues such as his friend, Roger Gale, the astronomer, Edmond Halley, and the noblemen Lords Pembroke and Winchelsea, he measured, planned, examined the diverse mineralogy of the stones, excavated, devised the word 'trilithon' and discovered unsuspected features of the landscape such as the avenue and the cursus.

Before that fieldwork there had been four books about Stonehenge by other writers, one by Inigo Jones in 1655, another by Walter Charleton in 1663. They were valueless, Jones arguing that Stonehenge was Roman, Charleton that it was Danish. A third by John Webb, 1665, defended the Roman improbabilities of his relative, Jones. The fourth, Robert Gay's book of the early 1660s, was archaeological lunacy, claiming that Stonehenge was built by giants. The only sensible research before Stukeley had been the notes of John Aubrey who planned the site in 1666, detected the Aubrey Holes and made notes of the surrounding barrows.

Fifty years later Stukeley was noticing even more unconsidered details of Stonehenge by his careful examination of architectural features such as the manner in which the smoother sides of the sarsens faced inwards to improve the interior of his 'magnificent temple'. The manuscript, therefore, provides an assessment of Stukeley's unbiased fieldwork before his ordination into the Church of England in 1729.

Stukeley, however, had a problem for which he could have no solution. His field observations were good but they were written in a historical vacuum. There was not one piece of information about the period in pre-historic Britain when Stonehenge was built.

Scholars of the early Middle Ages thought that giants were responsible for the immense monument. Henry of Huntingdon was more sensible, astonished that 'stones of extraordinary dimensions are raised on columns, and others fixed above, like lintels of immense portals, and no one has been able to discover by what mechanism such vast masses of stone were elevated, or for what purpose they were designed'. A decade or so later Geoffrey of Monmouth explained. The wizard Merlin 'had carried the great blocks from Ireland for a cenotaph in memory of massacred Saxons'.[7]

This remained a popular theory for five hundred years until the realism of the seventeenth century acknowledged a historical dilemma. 'These Antiquities', wrote John Aubrey, 'are so old that no Bookes doe reach them'. They were like the fragments of a shipwreck 'so that the retrieving of these forgotten things from oblivion in some sort resembles the Art of a Conjurer'.

Even earlier than Aubrey, William Camden had been sceptical about attempts to recover information about the unwritten years of prehistoric Britain from the writings of classical authors: 'I feare me greatly, that no man is able to fetch out the truth, so deeply plunged within the winding revolutions of so many ages . . . they lie so hidden in the utmost nooke and secretest closet of Antiquitie, as it were in a most thicke wood, where no pathwaies are to be seene . . . oblivion hath so long removed out of sight of our ancestors'.[8]

Fifty years later Stukeley remained in the same chronological wilderness. Even the age of the world was uncertain. James Ussher, seventeenth-century archbishop of Armagh, had calculated a date of 4004 BC. A contemporary, John Lightfoot, vice-chancellor of Cambridge University, refined it, suggesting that the earth had been 'created by the Trinity on October 23, 4004 BC at nine o'clock in the morning', an hour that very conveniently, smiled Glyn Daniel, coincided with the onset of the Michaelmas term and the beginning of the university year.[9]

Ussher and Lightfoot were not the first chronologists. In the Middle Ages scholars had been adding together the Biblical longevities of semi-immortals like Adam, Methuselah and Noah to decide on a Creation that occurred around 4000 BC. In 'As You Like It', written fifty years before Ussher, Shakespeare had Rosalind say, 'The poor world is almost six thousand years old'.[10]

Stukeley understood that Stonehenge had to be many centuries later than 4000 BC but the only records about ancient Britain available to him were of little use, reaching back no earlier than a vague 100 BC. *The Gallic Wars* of Julius Caesar provided some information, much of it unwelcome to a researcher looking for proof of a gentle priesthood.

The druids, Caesar recorded, were law-givers who held public and private sacrifices, a practice entirely abhorrent to an eighteenth-century scholar. There was worse. 'All the Britons do indeed dye themselves with woad' and 'groups of ten or twelve men have wives together in common', a marital practice quite unacceptable to an eighteenth-century Christian.

Even these glimpses of an undesirable society were inadequate. Around AD 78 Tacitus in his 'Agricola', a section of his *On Britain and Germany*, was pessimistic. 'Who the first inhabitants of Britain were, whether natives or immigrants, remains obscure; one must remember we are dealing with barbarians'.[11]

Of facts and dates there was nothing. And no one mentioned Stonehenge. That was in the late first century AD. A millennium and a half later John Aubrey was more positive. Stonehenge was one of many stone circles in these islands and 'Tis odds that these ancient Monuments . . . were Temples of the Priests of the most eminent Order, viz., *Druids*, and it is strongly to be presumed, that Aubury, Stoneheng &c. are as ancient as those times' before the Danes, Saxons and Romans, none of whom had reached those remote parts of Britain where there were other megalithic rings. Of the earlier societies of Stonehenge Aubrey added, probably to the indignation of Stukeley, the Britons 'were 2 or 3 degrees less salvage than the Americans' (Plate 8). Then the realistic Aubrey added sadly, 'there is no way to retrive them but by comparative antiquity'.[12] That seductive tantalus of classical history was followed futilely by Stukeley.

Being pre-Roman obviously excluded christianity but it did imply that classical authors might provide ethnographic parallels between known ancient societies in lands like Greece, Egypt, Persia as well as Rome and the unknown communities of Britain. Stukeley ransacked such writers for their descriptions of warfare, sometimes misleadingly, often utterly wrongly, for example when describing war-horses that in Britain at the time of Stonehenge were not thundering military steeds for armoured warriors and chariots but animals no larger than Shetland ponies.

He used burial-customs, marriages, farming, architectural practices that accounted for the engineering of Stonehenge and, above all, he inhabited Stonehenge with druids, the builders and users of Stonehenge. Neither in Part I or II of his 'History of the Temples of the Antient Celts' did Stukeley call them proto-christians.

To Aubrey the druids had been law-givers, prophets who inhabited oak groves and sacrificed human beings as part of their religion. And to the early Stukeley of 1719–24 they were the same, priests of Britain living before the advent of Christianity. By 1729 he had changed his mind. Druids had become proselytising missionaries preparing the way for Christianity.

It follows that in the early manuscript presented here one finds reliable accounts of unbiased fieldwork at Stonehenge: measurements, deductions, discoveries and excavations, all good material constantly mingling with a desperate search for descriptions of classical practices in Egypt, Greece and Rome that might provide parallels for life in the unknown land of pre-Roman Britain.

Despite the handicap of having no reliable time-scale, Stukeley's work does mark a watershed in antiquarian studies. He was no longer utterly dependent upon classical sources for comparisons although many of his conclusions did contain literary references to buttress his practical field-work. It was an inevitable combination. Like his predecessors Stukeley had no information about indigenous prehistory. It is to his credit that in his early notes about Stonehenge personal observations usually took prece-dence over classical sources.

He changed. His *Stonehenge* of 1740, is half a sensible description of what could be seen in the ring and its surroundings and half a distorted and unconvincing piece of propaganda against the theological free-thinkers of the mid-eighteenth century. His Stonehenge druids became proto-Christians. The text in the present book has none of this. Among other considerations the transcription provides justice for an unfairly maligned, clear-headed fieldworker who has too frequently been judged only on the contents of his published books.

Although Stukeley did include the contents of the manuscript in his pub-lished volume *Stonehenge* in 1740, that book had serious demerits. He had become obsessed with pseudo-Druidism and after he took holy orders in 1729 he deliberately used Stonehenge and the great circle of Avebury to prove his own theories about primitive religion. A few years after his book about Stonehenge had been published he said so in a letter to William Wake, Archbishop of Canterbury, who had encouraged him to take holy orders,

Stamford jan. 1. 1746/7.
Most Reverend, my good Lord.
　　I found myself indispensably oblig'd, to answer your Graces kind letter, & to return my most humble thanks for your good opinion of my book.

in truth my view of it at the bottom, was religious. & I think it behoves us to catch at any opportunity that may possibly draw mankind, from their present thoughtless humor about their greatest concern. The good impressions I received at college, were too deep rooted ever to be effac'd, by my long converse, among the Hippocratic gentlemen. & tis many years ago, that I turn'd all the little knowledge I had acquir'd in antiquity – matters intirely towards religious views.[13]

Stukeley falsified measurements and plans at Avebury to fit these notions. Rickman complained, 'nothing can exceed the effrontery with which Stukeley inserted curved avenues between these circles [at Stanton Drew], so as to make the whole into a serpent form. Nothing of the kind exists'. His books on Avebury and Stonehenge are half clear and objective records of his fieldwork, and half nonsensical jumbles from his later years. Piggott commented on this distinct difference between the quality of his notes before 1725 and his eccentric thinking after that year.[14]

Piggott's conclusions have been questioned: 'This fundamental inaccuracy', according to Haycock. There were other critics. Hunter dismissed the belief in Stukeley's change of mind as 'a *chiasma* which has no factual basis', and Ucko and colleagues observed that in Stukeley's work, early or late, 'the Druids constantly reappear'.[15] That is true, but it is misleading. The historically pagan druids of the manuscript do reappear years later but radically altered into gentle druids that never were.

Stukeley changed from a dispassionate archaeologist in 1724 into a religious polemicist over the following years. In June 1729 when he was requesting permission to be ordained into the Church of England he wrote to Archbishop William Wake saying that he had developed some notions about the Doctrine of the Trinity and the understanding that the 'antient Egyptians, Plato, our old Druids, and all the heathen philosophers had of this divine truth'.[16]

A seemingly significant quotation from Stukeley's 'Celtic temples' of c. 1724 that the druids provided 'the largest draught of the trinity' referred not to the Christian Father, Son and Holy Ghost but to Stukeley's vision of Avebury being a landscaped sacred snake of prehistoric times whose body was the circle, the avenues its neck and tail, and the Sanctuary stone circles its head, a chimera of the gods of ancient Egypt far removed from the true Trinity of God, Christ and the Holy Ghost.[17] Stukeley termed such snakes *dracontia* from the Latin, *draco*, a kind of serpent or dragon.

Nevertheless, the historians may be correct and Piggott, the archaeologist, mistaken. All that the present writer, also an archaeologist, can say is that he can find no overt evidence for Stukeley's pre-1729 druidical or *dracontial* credulity in any of the existing literature, whether in the detailed fieldwork notes here or in the abundant letters. Reading between the lines often results in staring at blank spaces but absence of evidence should not be interpreted as evidence of absence so the question must be left unresolved.

Even so, there is a hint that Piggott may have been correct. There is some chronological evidence that Stukeley's transformation of druids into proto-Christians occurred later than 1724. In the present manuscript he first mentioned serpents in remarks about ancient Egypt when referring to the gods Ptah and Amun, 'a primeval deity in the form of the serpent *Kematef*'. Stukeley misnamed it *Emepli* or *Hemptha*. Cleopatra, herself a personification of the sacred serpent, chose death through the fangs of an asp. Stukeley became convinced that such animals embodied the origins of religion. He used them to explain the design of Avebury.[18]

Stukeley was fieldworking at Avebury between 1719 and 1724. His notes were objective. But by 1743 and the publication of his *Abury*, 'a more particular account of the first and patriarchal religion' the circles and avenues became an image of a landscaped serpent, 'a circle with wings, and a snake proceeding from it'. Its ovate head was another stone circle: 'The HAKPEN or snakes head temple on Overton hill calld the Sanctuary'. The religious change from objectivity in the 1720s to doctrinal persuasion in the 1740s is revealed in his changing treatment of the Sanctuary. As Piggott observed, 'His published plan of the Sanctuary shows them not as circles but as ovals . . . but it is fortunate that in the Bodleian there are two original field-sketches of the plan, and in both the circles are drawn **as** circles'.[19] The genuine circles had been transformed by Stukeley into a semblance of a snake's head. By the time that *Abury* was published in 1743 the archaeologist had been transformed into a propagandist for the doctrines of the Anglican Church.

Why Stukeley entered holy orders, his friends thinking him crazy, and why he transformed the druids may in part be attributed to two influences, the Arianism of William Whiston, and the arguments of freethinkers such as William Whiston and John Toland, both of whom doubted that the first Christians believed in the Trinity but rather in a single, all-powerful God.

Whiston, a mathematician who had studied Newton's *Principia*, took holy orders, was then appointed Professor of Mathematics at Cambridge University in 1701, succeeding Isaac Newton. He became interested in early church history and by 1708 was suspected of Arianism, the belief that early Christians believed in the unity of the Godhead and had no concept of the

Trinity and the divinity of Christ. It was anathema to traditionalists. In October 1710 Whiston was deprived of his chair and banished from the university. Impenitent, in 1711 he challengingly published his *Primitive Religion Revived*. Despite having many covert supporters including Newton, he provoked antagonism, especially from traditionalists such as Stukeley would become. In 1720 he hoped to be elected a Fellow of the Royal Society but the President, none other than Sir Isaac Newton, 'refused his admittance'.[20]

As well as Whiston's heresies there was the posthumous publication in 1726 of John Toland's *A Critical History of the Celtic Religion and Learning Containing an Account of the Druids*. Stukeley had been given the two volumes by his friend William Warburton in 1729. In them Toland discussed stone circles: 'tis certain that all those nations meant by those stones without statues [was] the eternal stability and power of the Deity'.

Toland was a Deist whose *Christianity Most Mysterious* of 1696 was publicly burnt by the hangman in Dublin at the command of the House of Commons for being 'atheistical and subversive'. Toland had argued that 'because Christian revelation is from God and is therefore true, it must be rational and true'. It 'allowed the original, primitive, untutored to be presented as a rational being very like an educated 18th century gentleman in comfortable circumstances'.[21]

'Toland's studies in comparative religion led him to the Druids, and Stukeley's antagonism to what he conceived to be the Deistic doctrines led him to find in the half-forgotten Iron Age priesthood justification for his ideas on natural religion'. As his thoughts developed, Stukeley surmised that the ancestors of the druids had come from the east, *ex oriente lux*, 'light from the orient', spreading into western Europe, and were 'of *Abraham's* religion entirely', that is, pre-Christian.[22]

In his books of 1740 and 1743 Stukeley's hypothesis was imaginative. Tyrian Hercules, a mythical personage vaguely associated with Abraham, had reached Britain, erected the Cornish stone circle of Boscawen-Un and carried 'the reform'd patriarchal religion' into these Islands: 'Here, I suppose, the religion of *Abraham* remain'd pure, for many ages, under the Druids'. Their religion was 'so extremely like Christianity, that in effect it differ'd from it only in this; they believed in a Messiah who was to come into this world, as we believe in him that is come'. The ancients understood 'the doctrinal personalities in the deity . . . those minds that were of contemplative turn would embrace it and cultivate it . . . and of such a turn were our Druids'.[23]

It was nonsense. But the nonsense of 1729, 1740 and 1743 does not exist in the manuscript of 1719–24. There the druids were traditional priests and seers of pre-Roman Britain, and their conversion from pagans into the devout predecessors of Christianity was to wait for some years.

Stukeley admitted as much in an undated letter of 1729 to Roger Gale: 'When I lived at the University, & for some years in London, no one was more apparently & really religious than myself. The truth of the matter is that I had never considered those most important affairs, being hurryd too much by other kind of studys. But when the sweet tranquility of country retirement, & self conversation in a garden, had given me leave to look into my own mind, I soon discovered gain the latent seeds of religion, which God's holy spirit effectually revived in me . . . I really believe that my studys into the antiquitys of our Druids forwarded my religious intentions, for I think I can undeniably prove . . . that those religious philosophers had a perfect notion of the Trinity, God, Christ and the Holy Ghost'.[24]

It was probably only after 1729 and Stukeley's ordination into the Church of England that Stonehenge, the druids and Christianity became contemporaries. Perhaps for that reason, when his book about Stonehenge was published in 1740 he omitted any reference to stones in the avenue. His friend, Roger Gale, rebuked him for it. 'I think you have omitted a remarkable particular, which is that the avenue up to the chief entrance was formerly planted with great stones, opposite to each other, on the side banks of it, for I well remember we observed the holes where they had been fixt, when you and I surveyed the place'.[25]

At least five years before that letter, Stukeley clearly believed that the circle and its stone-lined avenue had been erected long before the Christian era. He and Gale had noticed the stoneholes. In his first 'Antient Temples' manuscript, there was an illuminating passage written before 1724. It provides firm evidence of his clear-headed archaeological thinking about those stones and their lack of any association with Christianity. The druids, he said, built Stonehenge. And they had built it before the birth of Christ.

'It may be reckond bold to assert an Avenue at Stonehenge when there is not one Stone left. but I did not invent it, having been able to measure the very intervals of almost every Stone. from the manifest hollows left in their stations and probably they were taken away when Christianity first prevaild here. Millions of Persons have traversed the ground over many times without ever discerning it . . . I am thro'ly convincd of my self: I dont wonder so much at the 99 which are gone as at the poor one remaining'.

This passage is doubly interesting. Unquestionably it reveals Stukeley's pre-Christian thinking about Stonehenge and the druids. It also demonstrates his keen archaeological eye. No previous fieldworker mentioned an avenue of stones. Inigo Jones in his *Stone-Heng* of 1655 never drew it. Nor, perhaps, did John Aubrey in 1666. A feasible explanation is that Jones and Aubrey were chiefly concerned with features inside the earthwork. The fact that both men did mention the very obvious Heel Stone outside the ring also implies that there was nothing else to see.

There had been earlier vandalism. Jones, who in 1620 had been ordered by James I to examine the circle and 'what possibly I could discover concerning this of *Stone-Heng*',[26] recorded four stones at the earthwork's north-eastern entrance: to the Slaughter Stone, Petrie's stone 95, just inside the entrance and its companion, 'E': and the two portals opposite them outside the bank, that 'lie so broken', wrote Jones, 'and ruind by time, that their proportion in height cannot be distinguisht, much lesse exactly measured'.[27]

Decades later John Aubrey found that one of the portals had gone. He was perceptive enough in the hot summer of 1666 to recognise the patches of dried grass where five holes, the 'cavities' named after him, had been dug to receive offerings and then backfilled but seemingly he did not search outside the henge for similar marks although his 'Ichonographie of Stoneheng as it remaines in the present yeare 1666' does show the remaining outer portal stone and two dotted lines, the Heel Stone on one, outside the entrance where the avenue would have been.[28]

Damage continued. Some half a century after Aubrey, Stukeley saw that the fragments of the other portal had been taken away. So had 'E', and the Slaughter Stone lay toppled, with a line of six 'plug and feather holes' in its north-east corner 'made with the intention of breaking off that portion of the stone'.[29]

Knowing of the former existence of those stones at the entrance it would not have been difficult for Stukeley and Gale to identify where they had stood. From the signs of the disturbed holes that no stone-robber had thought of tidying Stukeley would have known what to look for in the avenue, faint traces of weathered, overgrown pits from which sarsens had been dragged many years before 1620. Such stones would have been vulnerable, exposed on the open plain. Many of them were probably relatively small, as were many other avenue stones the farther they were from their stone circle. It was not until 1747 that the pillaging ceased: 'No stones are missing since Wood's plan in 1747'.[30]

Stukeley, having seen the great Slaughter Stone and noticing the Heel Stone, no. 96, some distance beyond the ring, probably detected two regularly spaced lines of grass-covered, shallow indentations within the banks that led to the entrance. Almost four centuries after Stukeley, Rodney Castleden ingeniously provided evidence that such an avenue had once existed, its stones spaced 31 yards (28.5 m) apart.[31] The late date from four radio-carbon determinations, corrected in calendar years to around 2400 BC, fits comfortably within the period when such extended approaches were also being erected elsewhere in Britain.[32]

It is a pleasure to record that after years of dismissal, even derision, Stukeley has been proved correct about the former existence of two avenues, the Beckhampton at Avebury, and now this one at Stonehenge. '*Iustitia omnibus*', he might have rejoiced, 'justice for all'.[33]

Concern that Stonehenge might been considered idolatrous may have caused a change of mind. In August 1721 Stukeley had drawn a plan of a stone-lined avenue with the prostrate Slaughter Stone, two fallen sarsens, the erect Heel Stone and the outlines of many other stones in two long lines not on but inside the earthen bank (Plate 3). Three years later they had gone. By 6 June 1724, in another plan, all the sarsens had disappeared except for the Heel Stone.

Stukeley thought that the outlying Heel Stone may have been a sacred pillar at which religious visitors bowed before entering the circle, because 'a part of the religious worship in patriarchal times, consisted in a solemn adoration, or those silent bowings: the first bowing might be perform'd at this stone'.[34] To have stones lining the holy avenue might have appeared too similar to the idols set up along the approaches to pagan temples. He eliminated them. He could not do the same at Avebury. The sarsens of the Kennet Avenue were still standing.

Stukeley can be praised unreservedly for the series of notes, plans, watercolours and the archaeological contents of his Stonehenge and Avebury books. Like Aubrey he noted details, but he noted more of them and he noted them more precisely. On his plans he recorded the dates when stones had been destroyed. He noticed that the sarsens had outer weathered and inner smoother faces; that it was usually the better side that faced the interior of the circles; and that the largest stones rose to the south-west (Plate 7).

His limited understanding of solar astronomy was further handicapped by an imperfect theodolite that prevented him from understanding the symbolism contained in the architecture of Stonehenge, a change from the lightness of day to the east where the sun rose to the darkness of night in the setting west. The transformation was obvious at Stonehenge. That ring's axis had first been aligned towards the north-east and the midsummer sunrise, only to be later reversed as the great sarsen trilithons rose one by one to the tallest at the south-west, framing the midwinter sunset.

Like Aubrey, Stukeley also had insights, wondering what unit of measurement his 'Druids' used when laying out Stonehenge. From over-optimistic arithmetic he proposed a Druid's Cubit of 20.8 inches (52.8 cm) used by the architects in staffs six cubits long, 10 ft 5 ins (3.2 m), anticipating modern alternatives such as Alexander Thom's Megalithic Yards of 2.72 ft (0.829 m).[35]

He even calculated a date for Stonehenge which inevitably, in the absence of stratified remains or detailed information about the age of pre-historic Britain, whether literary, archaeological or deduced from radio-carbon assays and calibration tables, was no more than optimistic guesswork based on false premises.

Among these obsessive misinterpretations Stukeley retained a sense of humour. In 1763, aged 76, when declining eyesight compelled him to wear spectacles, he gave a sermon on 30 October which he entitled 'For now we see through a glass, darkly'.[36]

He died on Sunday 3 March 1765, and it is an irony that his precise place of burial is as obscure as John Aubrey's is in the church of St. Mary Magdalen in Oxford.

At Stukeley's request, disdaining any vainglorious monument, he was interred in an unmarked grave on either the north or the south side of St Mary Magdalene churchyard in East Ham, Essex, near the Thames. It is the only surviving complete Norman building in London constructed as a parish church. It stands on a Saxon site. The churchyard of nine and a half acres is said to be the largest in England (Plate 10).[37]

Stukeley died of a stroke. A year or two earlier he had visited a friend, Joseph Sims, vicar of East Ham. 'When I die', he asked, 'may I have a grave under the green turf, and will you see to it that no stone or other memorial is raised above me?'

'In 1765 they brought him here by the Essex highway and over Bow Bridge, and laid him to rest in East Ham churchyard, levelling the grass so that no one could point out to the spot, and he lies unknown as he wished to lie'.[38]

Decades later a sexton's son was digging a deep grave when he came upon a coffin. On it was an embossed, beautifully ornamented brass plaque wrongly inscribed as:

Rev. Gulielmus Stukeley M. D.
Obit Tertes Die Mortii
1765
Aetatis su ae [suae] 77 ans

Stukeley had requested that Sims should be buried alongside him. Instead it was the vicar's wife, dying on 17 September 1768, whose coffin rested beside his. Joseph Sims, whose death was later, lay a few yards to the west.[39]

It is a fitting coincidence that, though their graves cannot be identified both John Aubrey in Oxford and William Stukeley in East Ham lie in the bounds of churches dedicated to St Mary Magdalene, patroness of students and men whose lives had been spent in contemplation.

Stonehenge

1723.

Great as were the Conceptions of the Founders of Abury. Yet
Stonehenge will not be dispensd with from claiming the second place
to it. Its materials are not altogether so extravagant in bulk, but its
neatness & improved Ornament with Drayton in his Polyolbion well
entitles it First Wonder of our Land. Song III.[1]

[preliminary page 2]

& most curious Antiquity of Great Brittain, & at present, as far as we
know only one of its sort in the World, therefore a most worthy topic
for hours of amusement & speculation, to recall into ones mind the
great pleasure & magnificent images which every curious & intelligent
person finds crowding in upon him, when nearly viewing so
admirable & in all respects so venerable a pile.

> *Seram ponderibus pronis tractura ruinam . . .*
> ['Wearied with storms, heels over with its weight, and threatens at
> last to crash in ruin; one portion falls by reason of the unceasing
> winds; another breaks away rotted by the rain, another consumed
> by the decay of years']
> Claudian, *Shorter Poem XXVII, xxxiii–v*, 'The Phoenix'.

[1]

That the same people founded both, was there any room to scruple I
shall show occasionally from the many conformitys & similitudes
between in the whole & in their parts, but most uncontestably in that
they are built by the same measure which I call cubit. & Wansdike
was the Boundary between them. For I see no reason to suppose it
drawn as a terminus between the Mercians & West Saxons, but rather
exceeds the Age of the Saxons themselves. It seems to be a Limit
between the powerful nation of the Belgæ that came over from the
Continent some considerable time before Cæsar & drove the Antient

Inhabitants more northward towards the Mediterranean parts. & this great ridg of hills which run East & West is the most natural barrier to be found hereabouts.

[preliminary page 2]

There can be little reason to doubt but that its British name was Gwahan which signifys seperatio, distinctio in D^r. Davis Welsh Dictionary from gwahanu to seperate, to which the Saxons added the termination dike from his high bank. That the Belgae made it, at least a southern people is plain from the rampart being southward & its keeping the highest ground all the way having the northern edg & descent of the hills before it, which adds to its strength. Supposing the building of Stonehenge more antient than the arrival of the Romans here of which I make no doubt, tis an indubitable mark of its antiquity that Wansdyke is between it & the place whence the stones were fetchd Marlborough Downs, & proves it to have been erected before the Belgae came over, because tis not likely upon the very fronteers they should attempt such a work or be permitted to bring the stones from an enemys Country. There must have been great & furious wars between them & the more antient Inhabitants who Disputed every inch of ground with them & for a very considerable time. This is evident from what I have observd in this Country as to their gradual advances from the seaside where they first landed which must have been on the south side the Island about the Isle of Wight & Portland. I have found no less than four

[2]

of their boundary ditches made from time to time as they carryed their settlements higher up into the Country. The first is in Dorsetshire north of Cranborne & seems to be the division between that County & the South part of Wiltshire by Cranborne Chase it runs towards Shaftesbury, having a deep ditch on the north side & proportionable vallum southward. The next is conspicuous upon Salisbury Plain as we pass from Wilton to Stonehenge about the two mile stone north of Wilton. It is drawn between the River Avon & the Willy [Wylye] from Dornford to Newton & so goes to Grovely Wood & how much farther I yet know not. The third is what we call properly the Wansdyke of great extent. These Belgæ doubtless came over hither a

considerable time before Cæsar & were firmly setled, Carvilius probably their king having advancd his royal seat as far towards their
frontiers as Wilton. For Cæsar observes II. De Bello Gallico that Diviaticus sometime before a powerful king of the Suessiones part of the
Belgæ had some footing in Britain no doubt by means of the people
hereabouts being of the same clan with his on the Continent. &
hither no doubt the princes of the Bellovaci in Gaul retird mentiond
after. Beavais [Bellovaci tribe] of Southampton.

Stonehenge then was in the Country of the Belgæ At that time but
what people of the former Britons inhabited it must be guessd at from
probably those that livd next it northward & consequently driven out
by the Belgæ & submitted to sett Wansdyke as their common limit.
Comius of Arras too no doubt had some interest & acquaintance with
these Atrebates.[2]

[1]

It begins above the Devizes & passes a little above Great Bedwyn tra-
versing Savernake Forest seperating the Belgæ from the Dobuni. Then
it enters Berkshire the territory of the Bibroci but its termination I
know not. These Belgæ came from about the mouth of the Rhine, &
considering the vast number of barrows all around Stonehenge if we
allow them the sepulchres of Kings & great Men, of which there is
little question, there seems not time enough for so many before the
Romans made the Britons conform to their modes.

D[r]. Halley upon sight of Stonehenge A°. 1720.[3] brought a good
argument for its antiquity (which I have heard him repeat) from the

[3]

wear of the weather, for says he, if we consider the Texture of the
stone which is not inferior to Marble in hardness & withal the effect
which continuance of time has brought upon it, we cannot reasonably
imagine it has stood less than 3000 years, & if need be may extend its
date much higher. The piece of stone which the D[r]. broke off was
from one of the stumps of a pyramid in the cell. I examind it with a
Microscope & find the rock seems to be that of St. Vincents quarry
near Bristol, tis a composition of chrystals of different colors red
green & white cemented together by natures art with opaque granules
or globules of flinty & stony matter, the Chrystals make up the major

23

part thereof are like except their bulk, those calld Bristol stones so
that in the whole it appears to the naked eye like a bright grey marble
hard & close & would bear a polish were it not for the stony particles
therein.[4] But the great stones at Stonehenge are of the same sort as
those of Avebury & Marlborough Downs of a lighter color & not so
hard, & are indeed more affected by the weather but not without sufficient solidity to establish the D[rs]. argument. Why they should use different stones from the rest for this internal row of pyramids & of a
harder texture as well as why the Altar Stone is different from the rest
seems plainly to regard their sacrifices by fire, for these stones will all
better resist its violence than the others. But I have in general observd
of all these kind of monuments that I have had opportunity to see
that they are exceedingly corroded by the weather tho' the most
durable stone that could be procurd. & with necessary abatement
for the difference of climates It has been judgd that the oldest
Antiquitys of Rome have scarce the like marks of decay as to that
cause.

   No doubt but this is an Argument of their Antiquity not to be over-
looked. & that has its full force in Stonehenge which is scituate upon
an Eminence wholly exposd to the insults of the air, rain & winds,
without any rebatement. But the current of so many centurys has
been more merciful than the insolence of rapacious hands, not
only in taking away great numbers of the stones, but in continually
breaking peices off by the rude & ignorant Vulgar. Which detestable
practise beyond dispute arose or at least gaind ground from the weak
notion of many. Who from the prodigious grandeur of the stones,
measuring the powers of our Ancestors by their own minuteness,
think they are factitious. Thus the learned Camden, could scarce
afford us 40 lines upon

[5]

this renowned monument, & half of them are about their being made
of fine sand cemented together by a glewy sort of matter[5] like those
monuments he had seen in Yorkshire by which he means the Devils
Arrows by Boroughbridge where he repeats this trifling notion. As for
his print It was drawn I dare be bold to say not by any person that
saw it but from his own verbal description, & may serve as well for
any thing else as Stonehenge, & from which tis more difficult to count

the stones than from the Original which other vulgar conceit the noble Sidney gives into who wrote his famous Arcadia at Wilton & no doubt was often upon this spot. Thus sings he, But so confusd that neither any eye

> can count them just, nor reason, reason try
> what force brought them to so unlikely ground.[6]

[4]

The reason of superstitious folly is owing to the fondness the vulgar have for any thing that looks like magic, & which probably the founders infusd into the people & with such success that its not yet got out of the head of people above the vulgar.

[5]

I think this Noble Peice of Work needs no better proof of its Antiquity than the little that has been said about it in Authors, It has no less baffled the wits of the learned than the teeth of Time. None of our most antient Historians treat of it, or speak as if they were afraid of it. Henry of Huntingdon[7], I. calls it too the second Wonder of Britain, but says no man knows how or why the stones were thither brought the most Antient Inhabitants before the Romans the Britons I mean have recourse to fable & magic to gild over their ignorance of the matter.

[4]

Poetically objected to it in the person of old Wansdike in Draytons *Polyolbion* p.40. Dullheap that thus thy head above the rest dost rear

> precisely yet not knowst, who first did place thee there
> But traytor basely turnd to Merlins Skill dost fly
> and with his magiques dost thy Makers truth belye
> Conspirator with time now grown so mean & poor
> comparing these his spirits, with those that went before.
> Yet rather art content thy builders praise to lose
> Than passed greatness should thy present wants disclose
> Ill did those mighty men to trust thee with their story
> that hast forgot their names who roard thee for their glory
> For all their wondrous cost, thou that hast served them so.
> What tis to trust to Tombs, by thee we easily know.

Tis to be feard the Druids in time lapsed in superstition augurys, soothsaying if not into idolatry. Especially when the people of the Continent made great settlements among em.

iuvat arua videre, ['to see altars with delight']

[5]

It appears to all so deeply immersd in the Mist of Antiquity, that as Alexander & Pompey, when they peepd into the sanctum sanctorum they see only a cloud. Some think it so nice a composure that nothing but a vitruvius could form it, others so inconsiderable that the barbarous, plundering, ravaging & destroying Danes performd it, as if those to whom we owe the Ruin of so many of our old Roman Towns with their Temples palaces & fine buildings included should employ themselves in building Stonehenge in a Country they had no great expectation of possessing long, & at a time when their utmost diligence was necessary to secure themselves.[8] However it was generally reckond a matter of great Moment for Merlin fetchd 'em out of Ireland, but that was not enough for like the Santa Casa by another remove they came originally from Africa, & why not worth while since they are of a Medicinal Virtue & there is not one stone but can perform Wonders in Physic as Geoffrey of Monmouths Author Romances. I believe these are most sensible of their healthful qualitys that breath the fine Air which comes over the delightful playns they stand in, & that inducement put me upon thoughts, of exploring their Use & Founders & their vicinity to the most noble seat of the second Carvilius. If the following sheets I have drawn up on that head can pass the examen of his most Acute judgement, the rest of the learned world, will without peradventure, think them not impertinent, & they know the great allowances to be given in matters of highest Antiquity, where he that conjectures best may

[7]

well be said to have done all that could be expected.

Stonehenge is scituate in the midst of those wide downs calld Salisbury Plain, between the Avon to the East & a brook that runs in to the Wylye on the West both which streams are planted thick with Villages on each side, enjoying the fertility of the low meadows thereupon, & defended from the weather by the hilly tracts on both sides. The people that inhabited hereabouts, no doubt, were the founders of this glorious piece of Antiquity. Who might be called a tribe of the Belgæ whose name is still preservd in the neighboring River the Wylye, & Carvilium now Wilton their Capital, conveniently seated in an angle of the union of that river & that which runs thro' my Lord Pembrokes garden. This is low ground but a fine hard gravel, enjoying health & at the same time the security of the Water, which was so much regarded of the Antient Britons. Tis about 6 miles from it southward, at equal distance is Salisbury & a mile nearer is Sorbiodum now Old Sarum a strong fortress of the Britons & after of the Romans. Past which runs the great military road calld Ikening Street from near Norwich to Dorchester. Very strait, & raisd into a high bank all the way, still very perfect in many places. The two before mentiond streams with winding arms almost half round encompass the Area of Stonehenge, comprehended within a circle of 4 miles diameter. All which is Downs, agreeably varyed into gentle acclivitys & declivitys, perfectly open & airy & full of funeral Monuments called Barrows of great diversity. & all within sight of our Temple. Almost two mile from it Eastward is a Town called Amesbury said to be so denominated from Aurelius Ambrosius a British King & no doubt of Roman Extract, after the Romans left our Island, at the time when the Saxons first began to obtain footing here. In this place was a very antient Nunnery[9] now the seat of Lord Bruce, & overagainst it on this side of the River is a large & strong Roman camp calld the Walls q.d. vallum. Said with probability to be that of the victoryus Vespasian upon his first landing in Britain, where by his fortunate conduct he pavd for himself a way to the Imperial Dignity. There are too hereabouts, other camps or vestigia of them, one westward of Stonehenge, another southward in the way to Wilton. Yansbury is thought too to retain part of Vespasians name.[10] Tis pretty to observe that the common road crossing Vespasians Camp by Amesbury which leads to the town was originally the prælorian way of the camp.

[6]

This is a glorious dispensation of nature where she has given all her store of blessings at once which in famous proverbs she has but interchangeably afforded to other countrys. I mean health & wealth for the Downs serve for pleasure & the great valleys upon the River off the richest land imaginable having the washings of the chalk hills all around continually descending upon them.

In the Lordship of west or left of Amesbury.

In time they might degenerate into new species of cruelty. The Roman historians mention it practisd among themselves even in Augustine's time.

[9]

barows

Across the Downs run several little ditches or boundarys. Near one calld Normanton Ditch upon plowing in A°. 1635 they found some very good pewter, as much as was sold for £5. Says Mr Aubrey.[11]

[8]

These ditches seem to have been made in the Saxon times for division of Lordships townships & the like one runs across the Bath road.

[9]

In the way to Amesbury are 7 barrows together[12] which are particularly remarkd. In one of them about 50 year agoe, upon opening it they found, coals of wood, goats & stags horns; the like I have known in several other Celtic Monuments. In another a shepherd took up a human skull very near the surface. But my Lord Pembroke causd this matter to be examind & upon opening sevral, they found a single body constantly.

[8]

This was some of the old Brittish Stannu. The tin of Tyre which those merchants of Greece bought at the fairs there mentiond Ezekiel XXIIII.12. But the midianites had got it long before from the Tyrians number XXXI.22. Before which time they had traded into Britain.

[9]

Some of these barrows are manifestly composd of two or three placd close together, perhaps of a Family or great Friends or Wives, who might be fond of having their bones rest near together. They are generally ditchd about & formd into an elegant bell-like shape, but sometime when two barrows are sett close to each other, one ditch encloses both.[13] Sometime near them is a circular trench with the graff inwards & a little rising in the middle, which probably was the interrment of some lower in dignity. Others think it an *Ustrinum* or place of burning, for tis pretty plain our Ancestors practisd both manners. & about the sheeppenning there are several barrows calld now the Kings Graves, which were encompassd with stones, not long since carryed away.

[8]

As Mr Aubrey says, then the only ones hereabouts of that sort.

[9]

Some of these Barrows were long, originally. Particularly one remark-ably large, north of Stonehenge & therefore calld Longbarrow. When Mr Roger Gale & I were here together, he counted 50 barrows at least in sight of Stonehenge. My Lord Pembroke cutt out an entire segment of one that is directly south of Stonehenge three quarters of a mile, the composition of the main bulk of the barrow was mold, being the superficies of the ground scimmd off for a large circuit round & over this a thin layer of chalk covering the whole, which was dug out of the circular trench surrounding it, the body lay not above 18 inches below the top & with the head directed towards Stonehenge that is the north.[14]

Sir Andrew Fountaine[15] has the celt found in north p. barrow.

[11]

Kind of Stone.

The particular spot of ground whereon Stonehenge stands is a large plain with a gentle declivity from the Southwest to the South & North-east, so that the soil which is chalky is perfectly dry & hard as experi-ence shows, when the infinite numbers of horses & coaches that every day thro' so many Centurys have been visiting the place, are not able to obliterate the track of the banks & ditches, for no water can possibly rest hereabouts. The Authors in that respect well regarding the sta-bility & perpetuity of their Work, for more than three quarters of the circuit around it you ascend from lower ground. & was it possible to imprint a like notion into the reader or convey an Idea of the wonder & pleasure felt upon our first rideing into it, we need not doubt of entertaining with a discourse of this sort. Which the nature of the subject promises to be barren enough, where we are in a worse case than if nothing had been wrote upon it because tis necessary to extri-cate our selves from the perplexitys they have thrown it into, from the false prepossessions they have given us, whilst some debase its genuine

beautys as much as others magnify them. D^r. Charlton must certainly
have a mean notion or very imperfect one of the thing preferring Mr
Camdens scheme to Inigo Jones p.13. who on the other hand as Mr
Aubrey well observes in pleasing him self in the retrieving a peice of
Architecture out of Vitruvius abuses his reader by a false scheme of
the whole work.[16] We must pursue then as well as we are able, the
commendable Medium, & once more work upon these rude rocks as
we may term them the only materials left & the only Archives whence
to extract their Intent & Origin tho' Time has torn off the smoothness
of their scantlings [proportions] & left only the gigantic vastness. But if
it be necessary to goe back to the quarry whence they were fetchd it
will be fit that we first remove the rubbish & clear the ground of
vulgar or learned Impediments that obstruct our easy procedure. As
for the universal notion or whimsy rather of their being factitious
stone, twil be lost time to trouble our selves therewith, they must needs
have a beam in their eye as big as the stones that upon sight of them
still think with the Ignorant Many. They are of the same kind of stone
the same grain, texture, color & composition as all the rest of this
Country those lying on Marlborough Downs

[10]

which Mr Jones upon examination affirms to be the same sort I dare
be bold to contradict, for they are a lime stone like that sort about the
Bath but not lying in so thin beds. Salisbury Cathedral & all the
churches & great houses in the country are built out of it much of
after kind than Stonehenge. But no doubt they were found out long
since the Romans time for the wall at Old Sarum is of a different
kind. . Upon Abury Chase are S^r. Robert Burtons weathers[17] as vulgarly calld, prodigiously great whence Stonehenge was fetchd with
Herculean labor this is beyond Marlborough 30 miles from Stonehenge. Great oysters found in Chilmark stone & other shells as in all
the hill tops & quarrys thereabouts. Many masons at my Ld Carltons
who had workd in Chilmark all their lives say this stone is nothing like
Stonehenge. Oyster shells dug up east of Amesbury & in all the
quarrys of this country & the same as those of Abury.

[11]

Mr Aubury says in his MSS. between Rockby [Rockley]

[13]

& Marlborough on the Downs lys a great Stone upon three lower in the way to Stonehenge & as if going thither from the grey weathers, for from hence all seem to be fetcht the holes appearing whence they were drawn. Another lys in the water at Figilden [Figheldean], the grain generally reddish. & we saw another of equal bulk ourselves in the cornfields west of that Town about three miles from Stonehenge, these were probably dropt by the way after the work was compleated. But in order to disengage our minds (Celtic Temples p.85.) (Inigo Jones & Charlton confuted.)

Variation

A.D. 1620 6° of variation East. 1692 6° West. Its revolution is about 700 years according to D^r. Halley.

1692

$\underline{700}$

992

$\underline{700}$

292 AUC. 1044

$\underline{700}$

344   So that if Halleys Hypothesis of the circuit of the variation be right, Stonehenge probably was built about the time of Malachi the last prophet of the Old Testament a little before Plato flourishd, about the time that the first star of Aries coincided with the 1st. degree about 400 years before our saviours time. Here comes in what is to be s^d. [said] about Diviaticus.

Our variation is East

1620			1634		
$\underline{700}$			$\underline{700}$		
920			934		
$\underline{700}$			$\underline{700}$		

AD   220 AUC. 4181 APJ. 972   AD.   234 AUC. 987

700   700$$700

272 AUC. 479 years$$287 ante X. 465.

before our saviours

birth.

& it requires so much time for so many barrows. Divitiacuss' time could not be 100 years before Cæsar.

$$650$$
$$272$$
$$\overline{378^{18}}$$

[15]

approach

At half a mile distance the appearance of Stonehenge is stately & awful. As you advance nearer especially up the Avenue, because that side is now most perfect; the greatness of its contour dilates its self into a vast curve, that fills the eye in an unusual & astonishing manner. Both as it is a round work & very great, being more in diameter than the outside of the cupola of S^t. Pauls, & from the crebrity [frequency] & varying apertures between each stone of the outer circle, casting many & great shades, & distinguishing the object into alternate lights mutually recommending each other as a good picture & preventing too much uniformity, both as they recede. Circular buildings certainly have a great advantage over those that are square, because their form pleases the eye more, is in its self of a larger & more regular Idea & on every side presents its self alike, the temples of the Greeks had a like effect from their colonnades & the crebrity of their intercolumniations when veiwd sideways & aslaunt [aslant], but in a foreright aspect had too much identity & from the angle did not give that agreeable change as you lengthen or shorten the distance which curve lines produce. Stonehenge of all circular buildings now upon the globe, which may be styled of one Order is the greatest

[14]

& deserves Theocritus his appellation *Deorum gloriosa domus,* ['house of the glorious gods'] as he & Herodutus often calls temples. Pausanias praises the Tanagrei in Beotia [Boetia] for having the temples of their gods distant from profane buildings & the traffic of men in a clean & distinct area.

This is the *campus sacor* as it may calld. As that in Egypt where Osiris & Isis were buryd Dio sic [Diodorus Siculus] I. 22.

[15]

This reasoning is very clear to those that have observd the Amphitheatres at Rome & elsewhere. Here above the outer circle you see the tops of the Cell like an Attick, & plainly demonstrating by the rules of perspective that there is an interior work, that tis not shell only. & this is well contrivd as it breaks the similarity of the upper line which otherwise would offend. But when you are near & see the mighty imposts stretchd over these great chasms from the middle of one stone of so vast a bredth to the middle of the other, & lying them together as an enormous cincture or girdle: when you ride thro' as in to the gate of a city & see but less than a third part only of those broad flat Architraves like Rocks pild up by Giants, hanging over your head when you see further the still more lofty & more bulky stones of the Cell, overlaid again with much greater Architraves: you must confess that nothing thats not as insensible as the stones, but will be movd exceedingly, or rather be struck with amazement & stand aghast as stedfast as they, rapt up in a most agreable reverie. After you recover that fitt, & cast your eyes around, here observing the great concave of a circular portico winding round you, divided with a circle of obelisks, or the aperture of the wings of the cell & its wide ellipsis,

[17]

there the larger obelisks withinside; when you survey each stone & the whole collectively & consider the forms, the parts thereof, their monstrous bulk their uses and design; when you see withal the rude havoc, the desolation the shattered bowels of quarrys turned inside outward, the fractures of Mountains toss't about, as if Nature had sported there, when you conjecture with your self about the means of erecting this stupendous pile, when you come to examin in your mind whether the work had more majesty in its perfection than in its haughty ruins: when you lift up your eyes & see so large a space of the blue convex defind into a circular hemisphere over you & making as it were a heavenly covering or *tholus* of the whole building; a mind that is to be affected with any thing will be apt to fancy its self in heaven, & in exstacy conclude these were Men of a great thought & worthy of perpetual memory. You will be apt to despise the Pyramids or the Obelisks of Ægypt which tho' great yet are but of simple dimensions, you will reckon Stonehenge a collection of wonders,

Seven in One. But after all, Words are too short to express the emotion & I refer you only to the work its self, whilst yet subsisting.

[16]

measure

Father Brothais in his Observation on Upper Egypt found a door case made of one stone $26\frac{1}{2}$ feet (8.1 m) long in height. this is 15 cubits. So D^r. Huntington in the Transactions says the Sphynx standing by the northern pyramids is 110 feet (33.5 m) in circuit i.e. 60 cubits the very measure Webb gives to the diameter of stonehenge. The Hebrew & Egyptian cubit was divided into 6 palms so was ours here. Vitruvius says so thus in the stones of the outer circle the base or perimeter of the semi spherical tenons or mortaises are something more than 10 inches in diameter. That is three palms or half a cubit. The interval between them is 6 feet i.e. 3 cubits & $\frac{1}{2}$ upon the imposts but in the uprights each tenon is from the other 2 feet 4 i.e. 1 cubit & 2 palms. So the impost over the grand entrance is in the middle 11 feet 11 long (3.6 m), 7 cubits, 4 palms. 2.10. high, 1 cubit 4 palms. The rest being but 1 cubit 3 palms or $1\frac{1}{2}$.

Thus says D^r. Arbuthnot the side of the Great Pyramid as mesurd by Greaves is 693 English feet (211 m) which in the Egyptian cubit comes to just 400, most undoubtedly the originally designd mesure. He adds many more deducd in the same way to confirm. I add, Greaves says the lowermost slops [slopes] of the pyramid are near 4 feet in height i.e. 2 cubits 2 palms 3 feet in British i.e. 1 cubit 4 palms. The length of the declining first entrance is 92 feet $\frac{1}{2}$ (28.2 m) i.e 55 cubits. The length of the next gallery is 110 feet (33.5 m) the very mesure Webb gives to the diameter of our antiquity Stonehenge. Tis 60 cubits. There is another gallery in the pyramid of the same length. & this is a comon mesure of our Druid works in Brittan as Rowldrich.[19]

Ptolemy iv. & Pliny xxxvi speaks of the obelisc raisd by King Ramesis at Heliopolis ['Ramses . . . erected one of 140 cubits'] which Mr Webb p.34 says 136 English feet (41.5 m) i.e 80 cubits, that which Augusta set up in the Great Circle at Rome he says 120.9. (36.9 m) which makes to speak in the eastern way 70 cubits. Another Augusta set up in the Camp de Mart[20] which he says was 9 feet higher i.e 5 cubits. He speaks again of that set up by Fontana before S^t. Peters at Rome 81 feet (24.7 m) high it wants a little of 50 cubits. I suppose it was broke off. At the base 9 feet square 5 cubits.

[17]

name

The name of this most notable Antiquity Stanehange or Stonehenge as now pronouncd, is plainly Saxon & signifys only the hanging stones, from the Architraves as seeming the greatest part of the Wonder, they hanging as it were in the air, which is an Argument that neither The Saxons or Danes built it, for then it would have had & retaind some more apposite name, expressive of the Person or uses it was raised for, & in Yorkshire, Pendulous rocks are now called Henges, & I have been informd that there is another place there calld Stonehenges, being natural rocks.[21]

[12]

Rode henzenne is a gallows, stone hengen among our Saxon ancestors is a stone gallows. The very Saxon name shows the Saxons not the authors.

[17]

The old British name is said to be Choir gaur, which some interpret Choræa Gigantum the Giants dance, but more rightly Chorus magnus the great Choir or Temple as Banchor is the high Temple. In D^r. Davis's Welsh dictionary Côr is chorus, whereas chorea is chwarae. & this is certainly from its circular form, whether the Latin or the British be the primitive. Isidore derives it from Corona, which in British is crwn, in Armoric cryn signifying *rotunudus*. *Kru* in Irish. Hence the synonymous *corddyn cardo, corwynt a topp, coryn* the round tip of any thing. & many other like words in all

[19]

the different Celtic Dialects. As for Geffrys [Geoffrey of Monmouth] name of Giants dance it has no relation to the purpose of the story,[22] for which it was mentiond. Chorus among the latest Romans was the circular building round east end the altar, the cheif place of worship & principal part of the temple. The rest were porticos' walks & courts or areas. As our cathedrals are now parcelld out. Cortona formerly

Coritus a city of the Celts in Umbria upon the top of a mountain doubtless so calld from its circular form, *Korol arm*. Chorea from turning round corolla a glirland [round-dance].

The general scituation of Stonehenge is not much unlike Abury for tho' upon rather higher ground yet tis placd in a theater as it were three mile diameter as my Lord Pembroke actually measurd it several ways, the tops of all the circumjacent hills or rather easy elevations are coverd are as it were with barrows, & cause a very fine & agreeable appeareance, adorning the bare downs with their regular & well turnd figures, scattered about without formality like the stars in the firmament, but yet chusing the highest ground near. & this ring of barrows reaches no further than hill you lose sight of the Temple, or thereabouts. The highest ground at the spot of Stonehenge is that directly west. For tis placd on the eastern tip of a ridg that runs East & West. Declining Eastward. Valleys on each hand. All the water that falls within the Area of the Temple will run to the Entrance being the lowest point. One may observe the stones, stand on a rather higher ground than the area. Visible more towards the entrance.

[18]

If we take a circular prospect begin at the entrance which descends gradually to the North East & then turns up to the right between the twice 7 barrows on the top of the eastern hill but directly before the strait part of the avenue is a long valley answering in a line with gentle acclivity to its length & ascending an apex which exactly terminates its visto. This crosses the eastern part of the cursus. Which there inclines to a southern plain & exhibits the appeareance of the whole race at that end. Beyond the 7 barrows the hill tops of [Dorset, deleted] shire are visible, at the bottom of which are many barrows. Between us & the 7 barrows is a deep valley which conveys the water of the whole plain even as far as northern long barrow in to Lake. On this side of it is a barrow[23] the nearest of all to Stonehenge. this valley goes southward, upon the next height is that fancyd to be the barrow of Aurelius Ambrosius.[24] Lesser ones underneath it. When Salisbury steeple presents its self there begins a chain of barrows reaching a 6th. part of the horizon to My Ld Pembrokes wood at Grovely & the barn in Berwick parish than the western height of the ground Stonehenge stands on eclipses a distant view with several barrows nearer hand now a colony of rabbitts. Then appears a little copse in the valley leading down the west side of the avenue than a many barrows at the west end of the cursus whose whole length is thence visible on this side the horizon with several barrows along the ridg that runs on its southern limbus which conducts us to the valley that crosses it at the bottom of the strait part of the avenue whose left wing is here receivd. Northern long barrow is the highest that way.

[21]

outer circle.

In laying down the ground plot & describing Stonehenge we see as clear as daylight that the whole is an imitation of Abury. & was made by the same people upon the same Celtic measure or cubit of the Hebrews. Tis obvious enough in reading Mr Webbs book[25] & which saves all trouble in a formal confutation that it is not built by the Roman measure, therefore cannot possibly be a Roman Work, but indeed that sentiment is so diametrically opposite to any tolerable probility in every particular that an ill naturd Critic would never desire a fairer opportunity of exerting his talent that way. & since he has given us the measure of the stones in English Feet & with exactness enough I shall accommodate entirely my description to the scale by which it was built & whence its symmetry is more easily discernible since in any other measures it must needs abound with fractions. We will begin with the Work its self or Temple properly, which well answers Donatus[26] his definition as being conspicuous, tis a place or space that has a prospect every where & which may be seen from all parts. The word contemplari illustrates this sense according to Festus Ennius[27] & the Antients call the heaveans by **_Temenos_** the name of *Templum* & *templa* are the upper rafters of buildings. The Antients when they went to take their Auspices by the flight of birds or the like, markd out a portion of the heavens by their rod which was calld a Temple in whose circuit the Aruspicer[28] took his lesson & this was done too with regard to the Cardinal points & hence comes our silly stories of witches & conjurers in circles

[20]

which seems derivd from the old Roman Aruspices or our own Druids.

[21]

Our Temple is the most perfect part of the Work, its outer Diameter
is 60 Celtic cubits[29] a third part of those Solar & Lunar Temples at
Abury and like them consists of 30 stones. Mr Webb says tis 110
English feet (33.5 m) but if we would be somewhat more exact tis 108
(32.9 m). That being the proportion between the English foot & cubit
60, the Roman foot is less than ours by somewhat more than a two &
thirtieth part.

[20]

We remember Greaves[30] tells us of two gallerys in the Great Pyramid
amid which he mesured each 110 feet (33.5 m).

[21]

Would not any one see immediately that the Founders intent here was
to use the round & full number of 60? Take Jones's measure & it
make $123\frac{1}{2}$ Roman. This outer circle of Stonehenge is formd by carrying 10 cubits 30 times round its inward upon a circler drawn in its
inward circumference thickness.

[20]

Tis reasonable to imagine the Druids designd to puzzle in making this
an oval. They call that a temple not only what may be shut up but
alsow is fencd in with pales stakes or the like as ropes a line &c. As
has been done for a time only. One reason why they sett Stonehenge
so far off the water was that wch has so long preferd it, that the place
should be uninhabitable. This country is like Egypt stretchd only on
both sides of the river above barren & heathy hence tho Ægyptians in
their hieroglyphs represented Egypt by an arm extended. the great
median vein was the Nile its mouths the fist. So all their great monuments &c were upon the barren part of the limits of the cultivated.

mesure

From the mesurs of the Pantheon do we not conclude that it was built
by the Romans. By the mesures of S^t. Pauls by English? Here therefore I must prepare the reader for a right understanding of this
noblest piece of antiquity by informing him that it is most indubitably
projected by the most antient known mesure now in the world, the
Hebrew or Egyptian cubit, the very same that the pyramids of Egypt,
& other their works, the Temple of Solomon & as I verily believe by

which the construction of Noahs Ark was performd. & by this mesure
I find all the works of the Druids in our island are performd. So that
we may deservedly pride our selves in possessing there visible monuments of the old mesure of the world. Bishop Cumberland shows
enough to satisfy us that the Egyyptian & Hebrew mesure was the
name, tho' he has not hit upon that mesure to a nicety. My friend Dr.
Arbuthnot[31] has been more successful in applying it to the pyramid &
the reader will find we have done the same in our works thro'out, so
as to leave

[21]

no possible room for doubt. The proportion between our English foot
& the sacred cubit as we ought to call it is this. The cubit is equal to
20 inches & $\frac{4}{5}$. Thus the side of the greatest pyramid at base as
measurd by the accurate Greaves was found to be [blank] feet[32] which
reducd to our cubit is exactly 400 a very proportionate mesure for
that square work p.16.

For tho' the diameter of a circle be about a third part of the circumference, yet this being properly a polygon of 30 sides, must be

[23]

outer circle

somewhat less than the outer circle when measurd upon strait lines by
the Compasses, or by a staff of 10 cubits, but this way it defines
exactly the centers of all the stones, & their bredths & the symmetry
of the whole, which tho' totally dissonant to any thing of the Romans
& their Orders of Architecture yet is very suitable to the design of
this Work, to its beauty & stability & was evidently done with all requisite judgment & accuracy. A 4th part of this interval of the centers
of two cubits exactly determins the thickness of these stones or the
bredth thereof upon the groundplot, between the inner & outer cir-
cumferences, markd in the Geometrical Projection Plate a.b. so that
divide this staff 10 Celtic cubits interval into parts, it demonstrates at
once the thickness of the stones, the bredth & the distance or vacuity
between each. The stones take up 4 cubits twice the remainder is the
vacuity, & all upon squares. The ichnography or base of the stones is
a double square, the vacuity a single one of the same dimensions, &
so quite round, but supposing withall that the curvity of the circle is

reducd into strait lines & likewise allowing the interval at the very
entrance to be somewhat wider than any other, which was as necessary as graceful, thro' which I suppose the Highpriest & chief personages present at the Religious ceremonies enterd. This is evidently so in
the building answering to the strait line upon which the whole is
founded, drawn from the upper end of the Cell[33] & high altar thro'
this entrance & directly thro' the gate & down the whole length of the
avenue, for it must be understood that here is but one chief Entrance

[22]

in the temple tho' every interval may be called such,

[23]

not three, as Webbs schemes suggest, to humor his imaginary triangles. There is nothing to countenance it in the Original, & he might
with equal reason have made 6 since so many points of his triangles
in his own figure meet in the interstices of this outer circle.

[22]

The base of each stone therefore is a double square the interval a
single which for stability & beauty withal is an admirable proportion,
but this is to be judgd only by those versd in the antient manner as
the Greeks built chiefly of low Doric pillars & small intercolumniations not like our common edifices now a days where the windows
are wider than the solid between them like Lanthorns, or where
pillars are sprouted up to a dozen diameters & as many for the
intercolumniation.

[23]

These stones are 14 feet 3 inch (4.3 m) in height, $8\frac{1}{2}$ cubits,

[22]

so that on the inside their bredth is half their heigth forming

[23]

that way too, a double Cube. But tis necessary that on the outside
they should be a little broader than on the inside as sett upon a circle
& these bredths defind by radii of that circle

[22]

therefore the outside bredth is exactly 7 to their imposts 2.7 high $1\frac{1}{2}$
cubits.

Very probably the Jews took a square form in sacred buildings in opposition to the round form of the heathens who at that time all about them & turnd 'em to idolatrous purposes.

[23]

This is reckond beside the tenons or what is underground. So that in view the thickness of the stone is half its bredth, the bredth is half its heith [height] & the interval is half the bredth of the stone & all this with great exactness, for those stones have all been squar'd tho' not with the preciseness of a Roman Mason yet abundantly true enough, that their scantlings [proportions] may easily be

[25]

outer circle

measurd thro'out. Its to be noted likewise that the tool has only been applyd to the part above ground for that buryed in the hard chalk upon which they stand most firmly is roung [rough] & unhewn as they came out of the quarry & generally 4 or 5 foot more additional length. this is very visible in the two great stones of the Cell[34] at the upper end behind the high Altar for one is thrown down & broke in the middle, the other leans awry & rests upon one of the pyramids of the cell which only prevents its falling, & the vast impost [lintel] of consequence is dislodgd from its airy seat & now lys upon the ground, here the roots as we may call them of the uprights are raisd halfway above ground & show the length that the chizel has gone most perfectly, like the appeareance of one of our stone or oaken posts sett in the streets to keep off Coaches.

[24]

The word Architrave [lintel] which has all along obtaind is here improperly applyd for what is a beam designd to but support so in truth tis to support the freez & cornish [cornice] & pediment or whatever is above it in Roman architecture but here is evidently nothing to be supported nor was any thing to be intended therefore it ought to be abolishd as its intent is quite of a different nature. In the room of it all along I make use of the word impost or cornish judging them much properer for tis manifestly a corona, but impost implys both architrave & cornish it has both use & beauty, as is our case. The

ⱷ the word architrave which has all along obtaind is here impro=
perly applyd for what is a beam design'd to but support so in truth
tis to support the freez & cornish & pediment or whatever is a=
bove it in roman architecture but here is evidently nothing to be
supported nor was any thing to be intended therefore it ought to be
abolished as its intent is quite of a different nature. in the room of
it all along I make use of the word impost or cornish judging them
much proper for tis manifestly a corona, but impost implys both
architrave & cornish it has both use & beauty, as is our case.
the diminishing of the uprights is admirably well contriued for o=
therwise the gynposts must have been much broader than
they [are] to have effected.

ⱷ being 3 cub. 4 pal. in the middle of the half of that or upp
face of the stone is a remarkable appearance being a tenon a
little above 10 inch diam. being an hemisphere or rather half
an egg in shape this mesure is 3 palms or ½ a cubit. the interval
betw. them is 6. [?]. or 3 cub ½.

＋ c are at bottom 10 inches diameter the space between them,
from inside to inside is 2. 4. the form of this is like half an
egg. 1 cub. 2 dig.

3 dig. or ¼ cub.

◇ within side & without
distance betw. out circle & out pyramidals 9 ½ f. from the
inner line to inner line is 6 cub. 4
the whole height of out circle with imposts is 16. 2 f. wch is precisely
cub.

× each of a circular form & 1 [?]f. diam. the imposts are a little
broader than in the middle than at each end to humor the curuity
of the outer circle. their thickness or height is two thirds of their
lesser bredth or at the ends a good proportion for the strength
& office necessary to them. their length or thickness is a 5th of
their medium length. theinner square in the groundplot of the
same plate shews their diminished face at top.

Pages 24 and 25 of the manuscript.

measurd thro' out. its to be noted likewise that the tool has only been applyd to the part aboveground for that buryed in the hard chalk upon which they stand most firmly is rough & un-hewn as they came out of the quarry & generally 4 or 5 foot more in length this is very visible in the two great stones of the Cell at the upper end behind the high altar for one is thrown down & broke in the middle, the other leans awry & rests upon one of the pyramids of the Cell which only pre-vents its falling, & the vast Architrave of consequence is dislodgd from its airy seat & now lys upon the ground, here the roots as we may call them of the uprights are raisd halfway above ground & show the length that the chizel has gone most perfectly, like the appearance of one of our Stone or oaken posts sett in the streets to keep off coaches. These stones of the outer circle diminish gracefully to 6 bellia foot breadth at top as Nature requires, so that the breadths of the Architraves being equal to the breadths of the upright stones at the foundation upon the Groundplot they proceed handsomely over their heads all as the capital of a pillar advances over the perpendicular of its shaft. In the upper part of those stones are two tenons or protuberances in the middle of each square that composes their upper face, contrivd to be receivd in the correspondent cavitys of the superincumbent Architraves. they have a circular base the Architraves are in length advancing from the middle of one upright stone to the middle of another where at a joint they meet, the ends of the next adjoyning on each hand their height is a little part of the height of the upright stones which is a 4th of their own length on the outer side. Divide their breadths into three squares & in the middle of the two outermost are the mortaises or cavitys that fall upon the above mentiond tenons & the middle one is left plain over the interstices be-tween the upright stones & this were they originally continud quite round as a bolt or bandage to this outer circle effectu-ally securing them from danger; & which no winds or tempests could have shaken, had irreligious hands abstaind & spard well nigh as much pains to disjoint any part of this monument as first erected it. the breadth of the grand entrance is 4 foot & be-cause the widest the architects took care the impost should be thicker than ordinarily as it broke over a greater interval & which shews great judgment & adjustment of weight & strength for they have thrown in this additional depth at bottom because at top it would be unseemly & break the level of the upper plane. hence this archimpost in that middle is 11. 11. long 2. 10 high 7 cub. 4. dig. l. 1 cub. 4 dig. high. as measurd in presence of L. Winchilsea by Abr. Sturgis an architect & my self. 3. f. 11. br. 2 cub. 1 palm.

diminish of the uprights is well introducd for otherwise the imposts must have been much broader than they to have projected.

[25]

These stones of the outer circle diminish gracefully to 6 feet bredth at top,

[24]

being 3 cubits 4 palms[35] in the middle of the half of that or upper face of the stone is a remarkable appearance being a tenon a little above 10 inch diameter being an hemisphere or rather half an egg in shape this mesure is 3 palms or $\frac{1}{2}$ a cubit. The interval between them is 6.1 or 3 cubits $\frac{1}{2}$,

[25]

as Nature requires, so that the bredths of the imposts or their plains being equal to the bredths of the imposts or upright stones at the foundation upon the Groundplot, they project handsomely over their heads within side & without as the capital of a pillar advances over the perpendicular of its shaft. In the upper part of these stones are two tenons or protuberances in the middle of each square that composes their upper face, contrivd to be receivd into the correspondent cavitys of the superincumbent imposts. They have a circular base.

[24]

& are at bottom 10 inches diameter 3 digits or $\frac{1}{2}$ cubit & the space between them, from inside to inside is 2.4 feet. The form of this is like half an egg 1 cubit 2 digits.

[25]

The imposts are in length in the medium part, advancing from the middle of one upright stone to the middle of another, where at a joint they meet the ends of the next adjoyning on each hand. Their heigth is so that both together make 15 foot (4.6m) high which is a 4th. of their own length on the outer side. Divide their bredths into three squares & in the middle of the two outermost are the mortaises or cavitys that fall upon the above mentiond tenons

[24]

each of a circular form & 1 foot diameter the imposts are a little broader in the middle than at each end to humor the curvity of the outer circle. Their thickness or height is two thirds of their lesser bredth or at the ends a good proportion for the strength & office necessary to them. Their heigth or thickness is a 5th. of their medium length. The inner square in the groundplot of the same plate shows their diminishd face at top.

[25]

The middle one is left plain over the interstices between the upright stones & thus were they originally continud quite round as a belt or bandage to this outer circle effectually securing them from danger, & which no winds or tempests could have shaken, had violence abstaind & spard well nigh as much pains to disjoint any part of this Monument as first erected it. The bredth of the grand entrance is 4 feet. & because the widest the Architects took care the impost should be thicker than ordinarily as stretchd over a greater interval & which shows great judgment & adjustment of weight & strength for they have thrown in this additional depth at bottom because at top it would be unseemly & break the level of the upper plane. Hence this impost in the middle is 11. 11 (3.6 m) long 2.10 high 7 cubits 4 length 1 cubit 4 high. As measurd in presence of Ld Winchilsea by Abraham Sturgis an architect[36] & myself. 3 feet 11. British 2 cubits 1 palm.

[24]

Distance between outer circle & outer pyramidals 9$\frac{1}{2}$ feet from the inner line to inner line is 6 cubits 1. The whole height of outer circle with imposts is 16.2 feet (14.9 m) which is precisely 10 cubits.

[27]

outer circle

Nothing in Nature could be of a more simple Idea than this vast circle of stones, & yet its effect is truly majestic, & venerable, which is the main requisite in sacred structures, & not a little heightned by its round figure, a single stone is a thing worthy of admiration, but the boldness & great relieve of the whole compages can only be rightfully understood in the Original & comprehended.

[26]

Joind thus by mortaise & tenon together with their own weight they are for ever secure from injury & winds & tempests & very difficultly disturbd by human hands.

[27]

I see but little reason to doubt of its highest Antiquity, & that tis at present the oldest work in the world where stones are thus laid across others as [architraves, deleted], none seem to come in competition with it but those magnificent Temples calld the ruins of Persepolis. Which are square, but the many figures cut there in basse relieve & the ornaments of mouldings carvd, intimate that Art was advancd somewhat beyond its first principles of pure plainness & strength. Besides their being square in my judgment argues their date much inferior to ours. For without dispute the round form was the first of Temples. Of this outer circle which has in its perfection consisted of threescore stones 30 uprights & 30 architraves, are 17 uprights left standing one toward the southwest end leans upon a [pyramidal, deleted] one there are 6 more lying upon the Ground whole or in pieces. Of the [Architraves, deleted] there are but 6 in their proper places & but two lying upon the ground so that there are no less than 22 of them carryed off.

[26]

I suppose this temple was thus defacd about Constantius time.[37] Eleven of the stones of the outward circle (uprights) are standing continuous, towards the entrance, five architraves upon them. Whence one may gather a very good notion of the whole. I am inclind to think the stones that are taken away were made use of for bridges over the fords of the neighboring Avon.

[27]

This is to be looked upon as the outer Walls or more properly the Portico of the Temple. When we enter in at the distance of 5 cubits

[26]

interval between the inside of the outer circle & outside of this is 5 cubits except the two jambs where its 9. These stones are not pyramidal[38] as Mr Jones makes them but flat parallelograms about 3 feet broad a little more than one thick so that they are designd for half the proportion every way of the outermost & therefore about 6 in height.

[27]

We meet with another concentric circle consisting of the number of 40 stones, tho now but 19 left[39], & a wonder any of them escapd

being of a less size & more manageable, 11 of them are standing in
situ. Whence only I fishd out their true number which is very ill represented in Jones's schemes, for to favor his Roman fashion he has set
them opposite to each upright of the outer circle & consequently
made their number equal to those being 30. But utterly repugnant to
reality, there are 5 in one place standing contiguous, three in another,
2 in another which sufficiently overthrow that notion. Beside in all
Celtic works they did not in the least observe that, but rather some
whole or particular numbers that had some relation probably to astronomical appearances. But then Mr Webb conscious that supposing
this to be as he would have it, yet would scarce be able to persuade
people that the Romans in making a Portico would have the pillars on
one side 10 times less than those

[29]
outer pyramidals

on the other, runs to the most wretched subterfuge, of Hermogenes (p.
69) inventing the *Pseudo dipteros*[40], whereby they contrivd (p. 78) very well
to make their Porticos more convenient being before too much crouded
up with pillars. Now the Porticos of the Antients were ever coverd
which was the very purpose of them, if the Pillars that supported this
covering were not of an immense bulk & their intercolumniations very
large by proportion & symmetry of the Order, they must necessary
obstruct the use of walking under them. Therefore Hermogenes
deservd well of Posterity who preservd the Ornament leaving a Pillar
on the outside answering to the row, but took away the whole row to
make more room withinside. But what has this to doe with our Temple
did they want room on Salisbury Plain, or have we reason to think they
did it to save charges. No if their Work had not been fully compleat
without it & answering perfectly the preconceivd scheme of the Artist,
they would have added more circles & larger stones, as we see at Abury,
but after all they never designd a roof therefore might sett the rows as
wide as they pleasd nor did they design a Portico where stone should
have answerd to stone they designd nothing more than a circle of forty
stones without regard to their opposition whether of the Pillasters as he
calls them p.78 or to the intercolumniations of the outer circle. & these
have no other respect therto than as they stand upon a concentric circle
& as every other part of the work, partake of some symmetrical pro-

portion so that they form a very pleasant & noble walk quite round, &
likewise it is to be observd the interval between them answering to the
entrance is wider than the rest[41]

[28]

& wider than that of the grand entrance unless part of the inside of
the stones has been knock off for they are $4\frac{1}{2}$ between. & they are sett
a little more retiring in ward than the rest of their proper circle, both
these propertys seem only the more eminently to distinguish this
interval as answering to the grand entrance that in going from the cell
back again to the area before the temple the high priest might not
mistake the directest & most commodious way.

[29]

And those two stones likewise so that make it are not of like figure
but broader & higher as it were the jambs of a Door, for more convenient passage up to the Altar.

[28]

Tis plain the design of making the inner circle of lesser stones was to
preserve a greater openess & at the same time exhibit the form of a
portico by lesser stones yet superior to a many heigth which is not
done by the *pseudo dipteros* to the view & semblance of those within
therfore in the Celtic manner exceeds the invention of Hermogenes &
deserves greater applause.

Any one may satisfy themselves they never were designd as pyramidal for behind the altar three or 4 are crouded together 5 times
broader now than thick, & if any thing be diminishd as doubtless
there is tis necessarily supposd to be from its bredth that the judicious
reader need not be apprehensive upon comparing my scheme of the
ground plot with what has been done – that I have made the inner
circle stones too broad.

This circle is made of pyramidal stones set at the interval of $3\frac{1}{2}$ cubits.
Webb says they are 6 feet high i.e. $3\frac{1}{2}$ cubits their height being equal
to their central distance.

[29]

Tis not worth mentioning to the Reader that there never were any
Architraves across the heads of these [pyramids, deleted], only
because tis an additional argument against Mr Webbs conceit, of the

pseudo dipteros. So that where there is no conformity in number, in shape, in magnitude, in scituation, in manner of the Architraves,

[31]
against Webb

in use or aspect, how can we conclude it otherwise than highly chimerical?

[30]

The geometry of this temple. No doubt but one great reason of the Founders, why they made the outer circles of an oval & whose excentricity is but 5 feet was that a radius of 50 (15.2 m) might strike the whole hundred or such a circle as should be thrice the length of the diameter, so to relaxit that a 10 feet rod applyd upon the inside should mark all the outerstones 30 in number. Tis plain they knew the proportion between a circle & its diameter & perhaps studyd the squaring it. But they perceived the proportion is not exact & that one is less than a third of the other. So the polygon of 30 being upon strait lines too must be less than the circle therefore they gave it the oval excentricity which dos it to the greatest exactness. Theres another great beauty observable as resulting from this disposition, that the diagonal lines which here goe upon the true east west north & south points to a nicety define the intervals between those stones, one coinciding without side the other with the other side.

[31]

The Temples of the Antients & Moderns too, had two parts, of different sanctity which we now call the Church & the quire. Fisly [firstly] designd for the station of the People & Priests, what we have hitherto been describing may goe under the name of the first. & what remains is the Cell or more Sacred place of oblation into which I suppose only the priests enterd. Thus the *sanctum sanctorum* of the Temple at Hierapolis had no door tho' none enterd there but the chief priests. In this part the Editor of *Stonehenge restord*,[42] has egregiously imposd upon us, & distorted it most unnaturally to humor the four equilateral triangles upon which he supposes the whole work is formd reducing this part into an Exagonal figure. An eye that has any judgment at first view sees its falsity & his own schemes demonstrate it sufficiently to any one that has not seen the Original, tho' he has endeavord to wrest 'em as much as possible to countenance that opinion, here is indeed five sides left of what we may call a curve figure three of which are standing intire composd of two stones each with an architrave at top one stone of another side is standing upright, & one stone of the remaining side leans awry so that here is enough left at once to try the truth of this circle by finding its center & carrying a line round to the circumference which abundantly disproves the proposition. If you doe this you see that the edges of some of these sides are no less than 7 foot distant from the verge of a circle that takes in those parts nearest the center. Again if you take a trigonometrical method & examin the intnal [internal] Angle in an exagon tis 120 degrees. Whereas in ours tis at least 150 as is evident in our scheme. As My Lord Pembroke Lord Winchilsea Mr Gale & my self have repeatedly done. Again to try it another way if you take the subtense of this angle in an exagon by a line drawn from the extremitys of two of these sides, & erecting a perpendicular upon it to the angle you find tis 10 foot whereas in our Antiquity tis in reality no more than about 5. & this difference is so great & notorious that an ordinary eye discovers it upon sight. Now our Editor supposes that one side of his hexagon is taken away entirely: this must be very strange without it had been done by Merlins Magic: for upon the ground & even in our groundplots you see no possible way thro' which it should have been carryd off, this side of the whole work being the most perfect of all not could three such great stones possibly be drawn thro the intervals of the others tho' a man could have carryed 'em edgwise as he may a brick or finall stone; or have lifted em quite over at top as out of a well. Tis manifest there

[33]
against Webb

is every stone & bit of a stone of both uprights & architrave of each of the five sides still upon the spot, tho two of the uprights fallen are broke in the middle & one of the architraves broke in three peices yet they are plainly to be seen & known. But that the whole of the other should be so cleanly vanishd exceeds any beleif.

[32]

The stones of the outer circle are 70 tun weight apeice.

Pausanias' *Attica*[43] speaks of a temple to Venus, in the front of which is a wall built of rude stone, nevertheless tis a famous work.

[33]

Again if we examine the space where this supposed side stood the base of his triangle, that is, the distance between the extremitys of the other remaining sides in one by his own scheme tis 32 foot (9.8 m), but in Nature tis 42 (12.8 m) . Examin the correspondent base of the opposite side in nature & you find it is $31\frac{1}{2}$ (9.6 m) which most evidently demonstrates that the Editors scheme is not conformable to verity & that the real figure of the cell is not, & never was designd for an hexagon, nor any other truly circular polygon. After all this observe, that the author himself was satisfyd, it was not fact. At first dash it must appear very absurd to place the work of this side the two great stones with their architrave directly in the front & line of the principal entrance. To what purpose is this entrance so remarkeably distinguishd from all others by the wideness of that interval answering to the north east point both in the outer circle & in the pyramidal circle[44] which looks down the very middle of the avenue & which tho' he knew nothing of the avenue he owns to be the most conspicuous entrance p.55.

[32]

& the intervals between the next stones on each side the grand entrance are manifestly crowded together to give room for the enlargement of the grand entrance as is obvious to a vulgar eye.

[33]

When at the same time here is the blank wall of this supposed side of the cell objected to it? & we know these two stones of the sides are sett so close together that a man cannot pass between 'em. This is hugely abhorrent of the Roman Architecture, & so far disagreeable to the Celtic that instead thereof they have expanded the wings or entrance of the Cell to about 40 feet (12.2 m) as we said before.

[32]

Indeed before ever I had seen Stonehenge, only from Loggans[45] two prints I made a model of it which satisfyd me it could not be an hexagon, & long since My Lord Pembroke & the first of any body, I

32

the stones of the out circle are 70 hun weight apeice.

Pausan. Attic. speakes of a temple to Venus, in the front of which is a wall built of rude stone, neverthelesse tis afamous worke.

the intervals between the next stones on each side the grand entrance are manifestly crouded together to give roome for the enlargement of the grand entrance as is obvious to a vulgar eye.

indeed before ever I had seen Stonehenge, only from Loggans two prints I made a model of it which satisfyd me it could not be an hexagon, & long since My Lord Penbroke & the first of any body, I beleive, by taking two or three judicious measures demonstrated the same.

~~...~~ ...ility. they found the regimen of their country in conformity to mee the heavens 30 days & a fraction the Sun thro a 12th part of his circuit. the menses muliebries and observant of 30 days or a solar sign.

Pages 32 and 33 of the manuscript.

is every stone & bit of a stone of both uprights & architrave of each
of the five sides still upon the spot, tho two of the uprights fallen
are broke in the middle & one of the architraves broke in three
peices yet they are plainly to be seen & known. but that the
whole of the other should be so cleanly vanisht exceeds any beleif.
again if we examine the space where this supposed side stood
the base of his triangle, that is, the distance between the ex-
remitys of the other remaining sides in one by his own
scheme tis 92 foot, but in Nature tis 42. examin the correspondent base of the opposite side in nature & you find it is 34½
which most evidently demonstrates that the Editors scheme is not
conformable to verity & that the real figure of the cell is
not, & never was designd for an hexagon, nor any other truly circular polygon. after all this observe, that the author himself was
satisfyd, it was not fact. at first dash it must appear very absurd
to place the work of this side the two great stones with their
architrave directly in the front & line of the principal entrance. to what purpose is this entrance so remarkeably distinguished
from all others by the widenefs of that interval answering
to the south east point both in the outer circle & in the pyramidal circle which looks down the very middle of the avenue
& which tho' he know nothing of the avenue he owns to be the
most conspicuous entrance p. 55. when at the same time here
is the blank wall of this supposed side of the cell objected
to it? & we know these two stones of the sides are sett so
close together that a man cannot pass between 'em. this is
hugely abhorrent of the Roman architecture, & so far disagreeable to the Gothic that instead thereof they have expanded
the wings or entrance of the cell to about 40 foot as we said before.
for so it is at present & so, I dare be bold to say it ever was
this whole side with its component stones with the four equilateral triangles must be banisht quite into non existence
as to this work, where I am sure they never were so much as
dreamt of. & to shew what I before asserted, that the author was
sensible of this rub in his way: in order to cure it as well as
he could & glofs it over from incurious eyes, he has turnd the
sides of his fancyd hexagon an entire sixth part of the com-
pas from their true & natural places, & consequently sett
the Altar against an angle or vacuity of the sides instead of
its true place directly answering the principal entrance, a-
gainst a side which is the upper end of the cell, therefore
every

beleive, by taking two or three judicious measures demonstrated the same.

They formd the regimen of their country in conformity to moon & the heavens 30 days & a fraction the Sun ran thro' a 12th. part of his circuit. The *menses muliebres*[46] are observant of 30 days or a solar sign.

[33]

For so it is at present & so, I dare be bold to say it ever was this whole side with its component stones with the four equilateral triangles must be banishd quite into non existence as to this work, where I am sure they never were so much as dreamt of. & to show what I before asserted, that the Author was sensible of this rub in his way: in order to cure it as well as he could & gloss it over from incurious eyes, he has turnd the sides of his fancyd hexagon an entire sixth part of the compass from their true & natural places, & consequently sett the altar against an angle or vacuity of the sides instead of its true place directly answering the principal entrance, against a side which is the upper end of the cell, therefore every

[35]
against Webb

part of the building is placd a sixth part different to the true point of the Compass, the north east which he confesses himself. Not only so but the outer circle & pyramidal circle, as if one wheel within another are turnd from the true parts of the included hexagon which they ought to respect. & in conformity to this error every one of the plates are drawn & wrested from the Truth. Tis notorious that when you goe thro' the principal entrance the high altar is directly before you & the side against which it is placd, & tho' in the groundplots this principal Entrance is not made wider than the other intervals, & in the second plate the Altar is omitted, to color the matter over a little yet in the 6th. & 7th. Plate[47] where the building is decribd as in its present condition: tis the most disingenuous representation that ever was offerd to the world. In the former plates where every thing was in its supposed original perfection, twas not so easy to discover the fallacy but in these the very stones cry out & disclaim so barefaced a forgery. Nor dos it avail to suppose that since his time many of the stones may have been carryed off & so disconcert his draughts, for if half the

stones were gone it would be but too easy to show the remainder is
taken from invention, but indeed whatever the author says p. 63 of
some being taken away in his time: I do not beleive it has sufferd the
least diminution since, more than little bits & chips which some
thoughtless people break off at angles & protuberant places with the
greatest difficulty. Nor have any been demolishd in the memory of
man, especially of the cell which is the main difference between us.
Tis very easy to find every stone he seas drawn tho' so distortedly in
both those last schemes, except some bits of architraves of the outer
circle lying still at top which I beleive is a blunder of the gravers, for
tis very unaccountable that the Architraves should not fall entirely
when the stone that supports one end of it is taken away.

[34]

I am the more confirmd in my sentiments that tis as he left it, because
all the pyramidal stones[48] as calld which are the smallest of all are
now left as he has markd 'em, & tis very necessary to suppose they
would goe first as easily transferrible. & some of those only he supposes absent from the first time he took his draughts. But there is one
pyramidal stone of the cell sett down *ex ingenio* tis only a peice of an
architrave which was split into three.[49]

[35]

I must own this is the most disagreeable office in the world to me &
which nothing but necessity has obligd me to. I shall therefore
descend to no more particulars. A lover of truth may be convincd
already. Such as are prejudicd by the greatness & worthy reputation of
its supposed Author, are only desired to take one measure when they
happen to be upon the spot, from plate 6. The two stones at bottom
is the principal Entrance or that which regards the Northeast, the
middlemost interval of the outer circle where three architraves are still
left contiguous. K.K.[50] are the two stones of the Pyramidal circle

[37]
Cell

which make its principal entrance correspondent to the other & which
I said are much broader & flatter than the rest. I desire the dubious to
measure the distance between that on the right hand & the great
stone of the cell next to it, forwards on the righthand, & standing

upright in the scheme taken with a pair of compasses & applyd to the
scale in plate 2. Which is applicable to this, you find tis 11 foot (3.4 m),
but in Stonehenge tis 26 (7.9 m). & so quite thro' but they that are not
satisfyd with this deserve pity.

[37]

So far have we gone in the body of our Cathedral, our pleasure
indeed has been somwhat abated by wrangling, but such walks as porticos & cloysters are proper for disputations. Now tis fitt with minds
perfectly free from passion, that we enter the adytum which the
Greeks calld Σnxos, the *concha templi* ['temple's shell'] from some
curvity generally therein, especially at the upper end, which has been
practisd ever since even thro' all ages of Christianity to this day, as in
the East end of S^t. Pauls. This fashion I am apt to believe the Christians borrowd from the Romans, for thus was Vespasians Temple of
Peace & many others as that at Antioch, Helena our Countrywoman
practisd it in her many stately Churches built in Judea.[51] So it is in
Santa Sophia. In our Chappel of the Tower & the like at Colchester,
both which if not by her, I am apt to think were built in her time. So
the Saxons constantly practisd upon their embracing Christianity as I
could instance in many particulars, tho' most of the Eastern ends of
their churches which were but small, have been reedifyd, where the
Normans have sometimes preserved the manner sometime not, as in
Westminster Abby, Peterburgh Cathedral &c. Thus the heathen
Temple of the Saxons at Godmundham in Yorkshire, by those that
have viewd its *vestigia*, is said to have been a semi circle, probably
divided into 7 *sacella* for their Gods denominator: of the days of the
week, & open at top as the Editor of Camden thinks, & surrounded
with a hedg & a ditch in imitation of the British ones. Mr Camden
well conjectures twas originally a famous Oracle or Temple of the
Britons as being the derivative of the Roman name of the place.[52] In
Edward I's time Eversden Monk of S^t. Edmundsbury tells us, in
laying the foundation of a new chappel there, they found the walls of
an old round church with the altar about the middle, which he supposes was that, first built by S^t. Edmund. Now whether it be true, or
that it was rather a temple of some Saxon Idol, or a Roman or a
more antient British it shows the custom of early time. So the first
temples of the Greeks were only a little *cupola* supported by half a

dozen pillars in the middle of a grove, or on the top of a hill, under which stood the

[39]

statue of the deity. Like wise the oldest temples of Rome such as that of Romulus were little round cells only, & many open at top, of which the Pantheon is a most magnificent improvement, & this method was probably derivd from the Tuscans, who were a branch of the Celts, so that the whole seems derivd from the utmost Antiquity of which the works we are now treating of, no doubt, were Prototypes. In Churches this semicircular part or Cove or Niche was reckond the most sacred place, there stood the high altar & there was the shrines & reliques of their Saints, perfectly analogous to this was the *Sanctum Sanctorum* of Solomons Temple tho' square, as the practise of the southern parts of the East, the reason of which we may perchance sometime discuss. But return we to our own work in order to show what it is & what it was, which is no difficult matter, since excepting some of the internal pyramidals there is not a stone of it gone as we said already. Therefore a true geometrical ground plot may be taken which was my method thro' the whole, & with all the strictness imaginable. That however I expatiate in writing of the uses, any person hereafter that thinks fit to treat upon the subject may depend upon the draughts & measures.

[36]

Open

In Arnobius VI.[53] speaking of the origin of temples, we don't says he make temples to the gods as if we designd to shelter them from the rain, the wind, the sun, but that we may therein present our selves before them, & by our prayers, after a sort speak to them as if present. Macrobius *Saturnalia* I. 18.[54]

[38]

In order to form the adytum take 20 cubits[55] from the center at the grand entrance **c** strike the ark **d e** that determins the aperture or jambs of the adytum **f g**. Take 12 cubits set it on the internal section of that ark & the principal ground line at **h** strike the ark than from the like center 12 foot (3.7 m) distant from this at **I** strike the ark **m n**. These two arks form'd into an ellipsis according to art from their two intersections as centers **o p** by drawing the segments **q r** from a radius of 24 cubits constitute the inner ground line of the cell or adytum the altar is placd just at the uppermost center at **1**.

Now this strait line from the Altar to the entrance is so obvious that whoever wrote Jones's book must wilfully distort it to make a hexagon.

The entrance into the adytum from one pyramidal to another is cubits 20 (6.1 m) feet.

The architraves of the trilithon are 3 cubits British.

The upper trilithon 12 cubits high beside impost. 24 foot (7.3 m). The impost 4.7 British 2 cubits 1. 3 feet high 2 cubits 7.1 British 4 cubits $\frac{1}{3}$. The uprights of the trilithons diminish outward & inward.

[40]
The uprights of the lower order of trilithons are 16.3 high (5 m) which is 10$\frac{1}{2}$ cubits 4.9 thick 3 cubits. The uprights of 2^d. order of trilithons 17.4 (5.3 m) 20 cubits high.

[41]
A trilithon is 15.10 (4.8 m) broad 10 cubits. The uprights of the upper trilithon are 7. $\frac{1}{2}$ 4 i.e. 4 $\frac{1}{2}$ cubits British. Just half much thick 13 cubits & a little more or 22.2 (6.8 m) long.

[39]
Cell

The *Adytum* of our Temple, is formd beyond any thing I have seen of the superlative Idea, & magnifys sufficiently the excellent understanding of the Founders. Had the altar been to be placd in the middle or center, no doubt but a circle had been the properest figure to enclose it, but this inconvenience generally attends around that it takes off all precedency & distinction of places. & consequently in this case must disturb the economy of their holy rites

[38]
where was an hierarchy. They usd to dance round here *tum Salii ad cantas* &c ['while priests of Mars to music'].

[39]
But with better judgment they placd it at the upper end that is not only the highest ground in reality but at the end farthest from the

entrance, so that from this altar you can look directly thro' the middle line of the avenue which descends all the way as we may stand at the east end of our Cathedrals & have a prospect down to the west door. There is no more room between this Altar & the Wall of the Cell than was necessary for the ministring priests to goe round, & by this means the whole area of the Cell is left free & disengaged for its proper uses. But moreover had the whole work of Stonehenge been formd of 4 concentric circles its formality & sameness would have been disagreable, & have savord of a poorness of thought, the like must be said of a hexagon or any polygon, which is in effect the same thing as a circle: & would have strangely diminishd the magnificence of this Pile. A semicircle or a square would have been horridly disproportionate if enclosd in a circular work, therefore have the founders rightly

[41]

pitchd upon the noble & beautiful orbit of an Ellipsis, whose excentricity is 20 feet (6.1 m) & whose *latum rectum* ['true width'] is 40 (12.2 m). So that the wings of it are defind by the arc of a circle whose radius is 43 feet (13.1 m). One end this Ellipsis being cut off for the Entrance it falls in very handsomly with the inner circle leaving at the nearest place a vacuum of 8 feet quite round. Thus all the heavenly bodys move in ellipses & thus Comets that have the most dreadful appeerance of all natures works doe the like, so the solemn & most awful aspect of this place, beyond all others is apt to put us into a religious composure of mind. The mighty stones it is framd of & the vast space it encloses, the agreeable figure tis founded upon, the long extent of its winding arms & the most spatious opening at the entrance render it the [proudest singularity, deleted] in the world. It certainly was their intent whoever composd it to refine upon Abury & in nothing more have they done it than in this cell, & particularly by introducing so artfully this ellipsis for here not only the formality of too many circles is avoyded as we said before, but tis an improvement upon the circle its self which for a temple no doubt is the finest figure in the world. Whereby the stiffness even of the circle is obviated by the perpetually varying curve of the ellipsis formd from the composended motion of a double radius, or the exquisite product of a triangle drawn round two centers

[40]

upon a plain or in solids by a cutt of a cylinder obliquely to its axis or the more wonderful section of a conic body. Or after the manner of that instrument they call a tramel.

They that never have been in Wiltshire need but consult my plate the view of the cell, for whose exactness I am under no apprehension of being responsible & they must needs perceive at first sight by the natural rules of perspective that another trilithon sett in the center upon the groundline would have no correspondence with the figure the rest stand upon in the line circle or angle but become a horrid eyesore to the whole.

The 5 trilithons of the cell seem to have relation to the [5 planets, deleted] two circles to [the moon and earth, deleted], a pantheon to the vulgar but to the Sun that overplus of the 100 Druids one god one altar one temple.

The transverse diameter & the conjugate are as 3 to 4. one reason why they affected the elliptic form was because it suited their conveniency best a long circle giving room for all the priests to officiate in proper places & according to their several dignitys & this seems to indicate the different orders of Druids bards Vates &c: & the internal stones were to mark their different stations.

The same opening of the compasses which from the centers **O** & **P** strike the outsides of the 4 trilithons below, transferd to the center **h** strikes the outside of upper trilithon & transferd to the center **ı** strikes the outside line of the 2 jambs of the pyramidal circle making that to define the ellipsis of the cell that way.

[41]

As soon as you have passed the grand entrance you meet the august view of the Cell which is presented in plate [blank] consisting of ten upright stones sett two & two, with five ponderous Imposts on their tops, so that the [Architraves, deleted] were not continued round as before, in which respect too the Founders have alterd their mode for greater beauty & diversity.

[40]

& thereby imitated Abury consisting of a stone & an interval between without an [architrave, deleted], nor could it well have been practisd, that distance in Abury being 15 foot, & in ours 10 which twice as much as the overture of the grand entrance so that a stone of this length between its bearing would have ever been in danger of breaking. In this place too there is a regard

[41]

to produce still a greater semblance of aperture in this more sacred part in which if any where they supposd their deity more immediately present, which ought not to be shut up in walls according to the notion of the Antients. The ichnography of this place being the major part of an ellipsis twice two of these ternary compages ['three parts'] are set on each side & one at the upper end fronting the Entrance of the whole & all this is done with great exactness so that the Author of the hexagon is altogether unexcusable in taking or rather coyning all his prints of this structure & falsifying the whole Projection.

[40]

For tis the most obvious thing in the world that the transverse diameter of this ellipsis which is the groundline of the whole reaching from the high altar to the extremest part of the middle of the avenue begins in the Middle of a compages [framework] as I am forcd to call it, or in our Authors style a side, not in an interval as he makes it.

[41]

The inner bredth of these stones are 7 feet equal to the external bredth of the stone: of the outer circle & half their heigth. Their thickness is half this bredth so that their base is composd of two squares. Two of

[43]
Cell

these stones are sett so near together that in the whole they compleat the bredth of 15 Celtic feet (4.6m), leaving the space of one Celtic foot between these two, therefore taken together equal one of the great stones at Abury both in bredth & thickness, so that they had undoubtedly that work in their eye, & tho' inferior in this respect as that is a single stone, yet our Founders have in the art abundantly supplyd that & gone beyond them, carrying these up to the heigth of 18 Celtic feet (5.5m) by which their proportion is more graceful.

[42]

& admitting the day between them & objecting part of the bottom of the imposts make an admirable variety of light & shadow.

Twas excellently well contrivd that the stones of the trilithons that compose the cell abate in proportions of bredth & thickness as they rise higher tho' tis by gentle & hitherto unobservd degrees. Likewise they advance in beauty as in height so that there is 3 degrees. the trilithon nearest the entrance is more rough, than the next but that in the front or upper end of the cell is finely hewn & admirably well taperd being most choice stone. This is just the same as is in the Greek orders, must we then say here are the three Doric ionic & corinthian. & they are by this means true imitations of them. I answer unworthy to be calld imitations, but is not commonsense to be found any where but in Greece? Is not the same reason of things and funda-mental principles of nature in Britain & as here they had most evidently an upper & a lower end of this structure in use as well as reality in the level of the ground, tis just they should distinguish it too by some more ornamental show of worthiness in its component parts. They that examin this matter upon the spot will easily discern the truth of the position but withal be fully Satisfyd tis an original & no imitation. It shows indeed how art advancd from one consideration to another till it gaind its heighest pitch in Greece whose excellent wits have reachd the apex because there is certain limit & extent in all parts of Nature beyond which we cannot goe.

The stones of the trilithon behind the altar are admirably fine & taper of 21 feet (6.4 m) besides tenon & root 7 feet four inch British which is 4 cubits $\frac{1}{2}$ 4 feet 9 thick 3 cubits 1. The impost is 16.1 feet (4.9 m) long 10 cubits 3 feet $\frac{1}{2}$ deep 2 cubits.

The Persians had this manner of laying a large stone across the top of two uprights as at Persepolis, so the Greeks. Malala the Historiogra-pher tells us that Theodosius the Constantinopolitan Emperor[56] gave the heathen Churches to the Christians particularly that great and famous one at Heliopolis calld Trilithon. I suppose remarkable for 3 extraordinary stones that composd the door as that of the Pantheon is of one stone.

[43]

These stones too as thos of the outer circle diminish handsomely till
at top they become 14 Celtic feet (4.3 m) broad taking both together so
that the architrave which equals in length the bredth of the whole
base, projects over their heads quite round, as a crown work or
cornish. This architrave too being of the same bredth with the thickness of the base in heigth, is a sixth part of the heigth of the uprights.
Which is the same proportion the architraves of the outer circle bear
to the stones that support them. The bredth of one stone at base is a
third part of the heigth of the whole. But its observable these upright
stones diminish much more on the inward edge whereby they respect
each other & especially towards the top, for there the upper face of
each stone is but 5 Celtic feet long. This was done with judgment &
for two reasons as I conceive 1. because by this means they have well
contrivd to lessen as much as was consistent with beauty, the great
weight towards the top which would endanger the oversetting so high
a stone when sett perpendicular. 2. that whence there is a square
vacuity left between their tops equal to the bredth of the architrave,
which gives us the opportunity of seeing all that quantity of the
bottom of the Architrave, whose vast & brown shadow adds much to
the majesty of the Cell & gives us a better notion of the bulk of the
Architraves mounted so high in the air, & which have contributed so
much towards giving its present name & this superfluity taken off the
inside of the uprights especially towards the top dos not offend the
eye in the least, or abate its good appearance any more than the
sudden cutt of an Ægyptian obelisk into an obtuse angle before came
to a point at top. In the middle of each upper face of thes stones is a
tenon of an oval form, which rises into a like cavity or mortaise in the
lower part of the Architrave, which by this means contributes as much
towards binding & retaining the two upright stones in their proper
places as they in supporting its prodigious weight. Here in these
tenons there is much difference from those of the outer circle, both in
shape & number the reason is very easy, they are managd very artfully
in both, as their respective uses require.

[45]
cell

In the Geometrical plate which I made to show these proportions
compard together, on each side is the profile as we may call it of the
stones of the outer circle & of the cell, that is their edg or thickness.
There we find them represented as columns of a real order, & they
have both the Doric proportion to great nicety, one is of five diameters the other of 6. & the architrave at top I have supposed as formd
into the capital. I wonder very much that our Editor did not happen
upon this, which would more effectually have servd his purpose than
all he has said beside towards proving this a Roman work. But this
shows no more than that our Celtic ancestors had due regard to symmetry in every part of this building, & in what light & manner soever
you take it. & that they refind their proportions with judgment as they
advancd more inward to the more worthy & ornamental part of the
building. As the Temple of Solomon was overlayd with pure gold, so
the *sanctum sanctorum* was overlaid with Gold of Parvaim which was
finer still.[57] Therefore the thickness of the base of the outer circle is
but a fifth of the whole height whereas that of the Cella is a sixth.
Nevertheless tis very likely that the beautiful Architecture of the
Antients which we call the Greek took its origin & proportions from
the like buildings to this, for this is the Doric proportion & no other,
which is undoubtedly most antient & most universally practisd by the
Greeks who never exceeded 6 diameters, whereas the Romans seldom
made less than seven too the former is the strict precept of Vitruvius.
& if any one pleases to fancy this the Tuscan, Vitruvius orders no
less than 7 diameters, for its heigth & the intercolumniation is three
diameters at least from his direction rightly understood but commonly
vastly more as Commentators assign it. III. 7.[58] & how monstrously
that differs from our building, let those judg that are fond of this
notion.

[44]

Of these compages if observd that they are not of equal height as
hitherto has been supposd but each is taller as they approach the
upper end of the cell thus thos two correspondent ones next the
entrance are [incomplete]

This great nicety observable in all the trilithons of the cell that they are broader below or towards the entrance the first pair being 15 feet (4.6m) the next 14 (4.3m). The uppermost 13 (4m). Exactly equal to the bredth of the stones at Aubury.

It requires no very nice eye to discern that the trilithons of the adytum are not of equal heigth, but rise in heigth & beauty toward the upper end. The upper trilithon uprights are 7 feet 3 British i.e. 4.3 palms leaving between the exactly 2 cubits interval 3 feet 9 thick 2 cubits 2 palms.[59]

I have a conceit that the lesser stones within the temple of Stonehenge were bound about with oak boughs during their great religious solemnitys for which reason their bulk is less. & so they made a wood even in the open downs. Hence Lucan

omnis [que] humanis lustrata cruoribus arbor,
['every tree was sprinkled with human gore']
Lucan, *Pharsalia, III, clv.*

& hence Maximus Tyrius mistake who thought the Gauls worshipd an oak for a deity.

Si qua venit sero magna ruina venit,
['the fall that comes late is a mighty fall']
Propertius, *Elegies, II, xxv,* 28.

In forming each trilithon the outside of each stone is chiefly regarded that it be upright & sightly the interval between them is but a cubit at bottom & widens higher, that by taking off the weight of the stone towards the top its stability may be better provided for.

Inner pyramidals 3 1 cubits 2 digits.

[45]

Of these five compages that compose our Cell the two of the wing on the left hand are perfect, that at the upperend is well nigh ruind which could have been done no otherways than by digging under the inside & taking away the binding of the earth so that the whole falling inwards the Architrave is tumbled upon the Altar Stone whole but seems to have broke the Altar in the half, one of the uprights is fallen flat upon the ground & broke into two peices the upper part lyes upon the end of

the Altar. The lowermost end that was in the ground is now half raisd
out of it & shows its broad rought pedestal un hewn, the other upright
which is a most noble stone well squard & without a flaw thro'out had
sufferd the like fate but one of the upward pyramidals timely opposd its
self & yet supports it in a reclind posture, upon whose tip its immense
weight rests its self[60] *quam super alta silex*, ['high above, them the stone
threatens to slip and fall upon those already down'] &

[47]

presents spectators with a new terror & often with a dreadful shelter
in a shower of rain, which forces 'em to run under its dubious cover-
ture. What hand the Duke of Buckinghams digging here in King
James the firsts time, as I suppose by Mr Webbs mentioning it p.
[blank] had in this overthrow[61] I cannot say or whether it was the
effect of some wretched curiosity or covetousness in searching behind
the Altar perhaps for hid treasure, or was it not a blind act of
Christian zeal to deface this stately monument of antientest superstiti-
tion? The next compages is still perfect the remaining one has one of
its uprights standing the other fallen & broke into two peices, the
Architrave is broke into three one of which Jones erroneously takes
for a stump of a pyramidal which he inlists into his remaining side of
the exagon but *invita Minerva* ['against wisdom'] it has none of its
measures, or place or the least shadow of belonging to such a thing,
lyes loos upon the surface where it first fell & much more inward than
the place where his supposed pyramidal should stand[62]. & which never
was in reality, as we have abundantly provd, as is easily discernible
to any one upon the spot that has but the least judgment. The Altar
Mr Jones has measurd for us 16 foot (4.9 m) long which is equal to 15
(4.6 m) so that it exactly equals in length the bredth of the *compages*
before which its sett directly fronting the great entrance so that the
transvers diameter of the Ellipsis cuts it into two bredthwise. He says
tis four foot broad so that in bredth & length it conforms its self
exactly to the base of a whole compages or of the Architrave both
which are equal. This is a slab of black marble lying flat upon the
ground, whereon no doubt the matter of their sacrifices was consumd
by fire. & by its positure at the very upper end of the cell left all its
hinder part about the center of the work perfectly free & disem-
barassd capable of holding a considerable number of people.[63]

[46]

Therefore the three uppermost compages encompassing the altar are most evidently modeld from Abury, the Cove in the circle, each compages here answering to a stone there which method having a stone in the back & one on each wing infinitely exceeds the invention of the Editor, who has placd it at an interval not answering the main groundline, nor the place it evidently possesses in the original.

The altar is $3\frac{1}{2}$ feet broad. Nicely squard 29 inches thick cubit & $\frac{1}{2}$. Tis very plain all the stones have been squard but not thr'oly [thoroughly] only where necessary for appearance & *secundum majus & minus* ['secondly, more or less . . .'] as more or less conspicuous or eminent the part of the temple is. The impost of the trilithon on the south side next the altar[64] is a most admirable stone & almost as perfect now as the first day of its elevation tis so glib & smooth at top that durst scarce venture to stand upon it. This is owing to the extream hardness of the stone. That of the other trilithon next it is much corroded Lord Winchilsea & I stood upon it together but 10 more might stand very conveniently upon it that stone when upon the top is of a surprizing magnitude.

5. July 1723. By Lord Pembrokes direction I causd a pit to be sunk on the inside of the altar at the middle of the stone. It was 4 feet long upon the edg of the stone & 6 feet forwards or towards the grand entrance. At a foot we came to the solid chalk mixt with flints which had never been dug we went 2 feet & $\frac{1}{2}$ perpendicular under the stone & found it perfectly solid chalk that never had been stird. I found the altar 20 inches thick, but broke into two or 3 pieces by the upright & architrave falling upon it.

We look up an axes both below the outside of the 1st. compages of the cell on the right hand.

> *Aedipus in mediis nudoque sub aetheris axe*
> ['In the middle of the palace and beneath the open arch of heaven was a huge altar']
>
> > Virgil, *Aeneid, II, dxii–xiii.*

At Æacêum within a septu is an altar just above the area, why they call it the monument of Æacus is a secret says Pausanias in *Argolicis.*

reccidit in solitam longo post tempore terram

['Back to the wonted earth after a long time it fell, revealing the
hurler's skill and strength combined']

Ovid, *Metamorphoses X, clxxx.*

[47]

The distance between inner pyramidals & inside of trilithons is one
cubit $\frac{1}{2}$ & whoever pleases may here measure the antient single cubit
of the Hebrews & Egypt. 3 cubits $1\frac{1}{3}$ measures the central intervals of
the inner pyramidals. So the numbers of the uprights of the 4 circles
make 10. 20. 30. 40 in the whole 100. But beside this, there was other
furniture of the Cell a similar circuit of pyramidal stones within as far
as appears conforming its self to the ellipsis of the greater[65] it is sett
about 3 feet more inwards, but by what I can find from its ruins draws
its self towards the upper end round the Altar into a [shorter, deleted]
ellipsis than the other. It is formd of an ellipsis that has 10 cubits
Celtic for its radius coincident with that of the greater & that 5 feet 2
inch carried round marks the station of its component stones consisting of the whole number of 20. For theres no ground to imagine they
ever came forwards towards the grand entrance more than to the
opening of the cell, only run parallel with the greater uprights. Nor
would it have been of any ornament to have advancd 'em further but
rather

[49]

cell

too much contracted the area of the Cell whos enlargement we have
seen so much provided for before. These stones are in bredth a third
part of the bredth of the great stones of the Cell, & a third part in
heigth of their heigth, the impost added, as was before observd of the
lesser outward circle in relation to the great & outer circle. So that in
every dimension thereof they aimd at a third proportion which is a
very beautiful one & a musical symmetry. These had no [architraves,
deleted]. Hereof are only six standing, there are the stumps of two
left at the South corner of the altar one lys behind the altar dug up
or thrown down by the fall of the upright stone of the compages
behind it & probably are buryed under it. One or two were probably
thrown down by the fall of that upright of the outermost compages of

the right hand wing of the cell. But I am apt to beleive we cannot err in the assignment of all the places of those that are vacant, as represented in our ichnography & in their number too.

[48]

All the cells about Abury are sett in this elliptical form & at other places. The inner pyramidals are at a medium 5 feet & almost $\frac{1}{2}$ which is just 4 cubits, the height of Moses's his curtains of his tabernacle.

Servius upon *Georgics III*[66] says in the middle of the temple was always the place dedicate to the deity the rest was only ornamental. The height of the outer circle compard to its shortest diameter or the whole front is less than a 7th. so that it bears a very good aspect & the upper trilithon behind the altar is less than a 5th. & the two other trilithons gradually lowering themselves present the effect of a noble pediment.

It requires 140 oxen to draw one stone 44 tun weight.

Diodorus speaking of Semiramis's most magnificent temple at Babylon says before the *3 images* was a table 40 feet (12.2 m) long 12 (3.7 m) broad which is near the proportion of our altar.

It must be ownd that they who had a notion that it was an unworthy thing to p'tend to confine the deity in room & space, could not easily invent a grander design that this for sacred purposes. Where space is indeed markd out & defin'd but with utmost freedom & openess where the variety of 4 difform circles p'sented its self to the eye continually now every step one took. Which way so ever we lookd art & nature mixt could avoyd creating a pleasing astonishment, very apposite to sacred places.

[49]

Thus have we finished the whole Work or principal part of this celebrated Wonder of Stonehenge, properly the Temple or more sacred structure, as it may deservedly be called, tho' its loftiest crest be composd but of one stone laid upon another. The four equilateral triangles being discarded, what other resemblances it has to Roman Architecture are so inconsiderable that D^r. Charlton whose skill in that science was none of the greatest, has sufficiently blown them away that it must be ownd more likely, that many of the Principles thereof were taken by the people whence the Romans learnt it from such like buildings as this, than that this should borrow any thing from them; nor was it necessary to fetch thos beautys how plain soever which we descry in it, from their more exalted taste. But it won't be too bold to say that in utmost probability this work of Stone-henge was subsisting when the Romans could boast of little or no skill at all this way. But then say some, is it not strange, that if these works stood in the times of the Romans when in a manner they were wholly Possessors of the Island, that they should not have left us in history the least account of them when many other odd things & inconsider-able wonders have not escapd their curiosity. If such enormous & gigantic forms as those of Abury & the like were disregarded as matters of huge strength only & indefatigable labor, yet Stonehenge that has such an appeareance of art & of a regular Genius, that is hewn into form & square ashlars [square-cut stones] tho' of immense bulk & that besides are cornished at top with stones of almost incre-dible dimensions which require mathematical & mechanical knowledg to rear them into their aerial slots & this done with exactness & sym-metry in the ichnographical design, in the orthography & final execu-tion; would certainly have arrested the attention of a people so

[51]
against Webb

well versd in these arts, & so busied in the exercise thereof as innu-merable remains of theirs now present here abundantly testify. Now at best it seems needless to answer to this negative argument which proves nothing at all.

[50]

For if only a bare supposal be taken for reason, then tis as easy to suppose the contrary.

Thus writes Clemens of Alexandria[67] if any one contemplates the fabric of the Mosai[n] tabernacle & what were in it with curiosity & prudence he will find that Moses a divine man in all thes matters rep-resented after a sort the nature of the whole universe. For it was nec-essary that he who intended to build a tabernacle made with hands to God the author of the world should take the similitude of thos things with which the world was fashiond by God. First therefore on this account he divided his admirable structur of the tabernacle into 3 parts viz. the vestible the temple & the inner adytum or the court the house & the adytum which might represent to us the university of the divine workmanship thus divided into 3 parts, or distinguishd into 3 worlds i.e. this sublunary world which we inhabit the next or celestial world & the supreme of all which the divines call Angelic, the Philosophers the intellectual. Thus then our area may be said to be analogous to the sublunary world as being open always lyable to showers to the suns heat & winters cold, in which the promiscuous rout conversd sacred & profane & in which all sorts of animals were brought & slain a vicissitude of life & death. Next the outer portico may be taken to resemble the planetary world, the 30 stations or entrances of the sun in the 30 degrees of a Zodiacal sign, here I suppose the inferior sort of priests were permitted to enter.

Whatsoever is great & noble in art must needs in some sort be copyd from nature. So temples imitate the system of the world.

The inner cove turnd into a great oval concave fitly [firstly] shadowd out the supreme residence or empyreum covering all things into which the high priest & the chief ministring priests entred.

[51]

I believe few Roman historians were in this Island, & what Architects were brought hither or bred up here who were most capable of giving a good account of 'em, probably seldom returnd to Rome, or might not chance to be familiar enough with an Historian to give them due intelligence thereof. As for the soldiery or common observers their descriptions would be as rude as what such sort of people who give in our days, whence a writer would have but little temptation to speak of them. But because we have so slender accounts of the Britons, & of their religious customs, must we conclude they had no Worship, no religion? Because they have given us no account of their language must we suppose they cannot speak? Because Cicero in two of his epistles tells us there was no silver of gold in the Island, must we believe it? Had they not silver and gold coyn & other ornaments of those metals many of which have been since found & are in the cabinets of Vertuosi. & dos not Cicero in another epistle contradict him self & say that Cæsar imposd a sum of money on them which they

were to pay. Which would be absurd had they none among them?
Great as the Romans were with sword & pen, we shall err to take all
they say strictly, or to credit nothing unsaid by them. Or that the
great work before us must needs be nothing, if not theirs, if not celebrated in their illustrious Annals, which were wrote to perpetuate
their own not the deeds of the Britons any farther than they con-
tribute to Roman glory. Thus their untameable courage, their high
disdain of slavery their camps, battles, chariots & their warlike discipline loses nothing, doubtless, in the recital, becaus it heightens the
superior valor & fortune of those that conquerd 'em, but what had
Stonehenge wonderful in it that was not seen at Rome, or when set in
competition to the visible magnificence of the Temple of Jupiter
Capitolinus of the Coliseum Pantheon & the like, & to what purpose
should they magnify this work of a people they calld barbarous, but
to depreciate their own domination in arts & sciences as well as
Empire? Besides have these authentic Authors wrote nothing but what
we see & read this present day, consider the changes of government
revolutions of Empire & languages, the ravage of War, fire, rapin[e]
& more devouring time, what vast desolation has accrud to learned
Antiquitys by the loss of our own antient British historys by the Saxon
conquerors, of the Roman by the Goths, by the burning the librarys
in Nero's time & the Emperors time, by the perishing of many valuable peices that never came

[53]
Romans

to our hands, especially such as related to Britain. As particularly all
the latter part of Livy, when our Country first became known to the
Roman World, so the *Bibliotheke historike* of Diodorus Siculus[68] is lost.
As like wise his 20 last books, where he treats of universal history to
Cæsars expedition into Britain. So all the later books of Polybius, so
Julius Rusticus his works about Britain & Xiphilin epitomizd by
Diodorus who was very particular herein. So four books of Tacitus his
Annals, so much regretted by all Scholars especially Britons. Who
knows what might have been deliverd in these, what light & inferences
might have been deducd therefrom for our purpose which now *ignoti
longa prenumtor nocte* ['now in a long night of ignorance']. But tis as

vain to raise an argument from their silence as to infer there never
was such a place as Rome, because never mentiond by Herodotus

[52]

or that Stonehenge was not existent in the time of Henry VIII,[69]
becaus innumerable historians of our own country before then have
not spoke one word of it.

The temple of Marnas at Gaza a heathen one was like Stonehenge
viz Reland. p.793. Stillingfleets Markolis.[70]

Such was the house that Samson pulld down on the Philistins.

Plinys books of the German wars mentiond by his Nephew of the
same name in his epistle to [incomplete] are lost & no doubt but a
vast loss to Celtic Antiquitys. Apollodorus wrote of the religious
customs of the Scythians Cavians & other barbarous nations Cl.
Alexand. in *proteptico ad gentes* ['beliefs of the people'], Arnobius IV,
Suidas. The 13 first books of Ammianus Marcellinus are lost. In one
he had treated particularly of Brittain as he tells us XXVII. 8.[71]

['I described . . . the situation of Britain, as well as my powers
permitted']

Ammianus Marcellinus, *History, XXVII, vii.*

[53]

After all when foreign testimonys were wanting we might possibly
have been able to have gatherd some what from home. Some tradition at least, some story handed down among the vulgar thro' all ages
which very often are of considerable moment in such antique
enquirys, if the Antient Britons after the Romans left 'em had not
been driven out of England with fire & sword by the Saxons, that
scarce a man of them was left not only living evidences but written
records whatever they had being totally destroyd in the Citys Towns &
Monasterys with a desolation like that of the Jews by Titus. As Henry
of Huntingdon among others gives us a very particular account, for
so says he the Victor Hengist depopulating all the neighboring citys &
fields, no one hindring continued his burning from the east sea even
to the west, & coverd the whole face of the perishing Island. The

public & private buildings fell together, & all was consumd by the
flames together with the people. The same Author tells us the Scots &
Picts much about the same time miserably ravagd the Kingdom &
destroyd all the Towns northward even as far as Stanford, so that
between both a finishing stroke was made of all memorials to our
purpose. All the old Brittish books were destroyd by the Saxons says
Cooper voce *Brittania.*[72] Who endeavord utterly to extinguish their
very name. So that the very appellatives of the old Citys, Rivers &
Countrys were for the most part forgotten & new ones applyd by the
Conquerors, otherwise we might resonably hope for some small light
thence, the names of some of the barrows round our structures, the
shadows of some superstitious customs & anniversarys & the like are
eternally vanishd, & there remains nothing to be done in the case but
for the monuments to declare their own storys with their languishing
& last breath. Nor are they under much worse circumstances than the
famous Antiquitys of other Countrys, how trifling are our informa-
tions concerning the pompous

[55]

ruins of Persepolis, of Tadmor, & innumerable antient citys in the
East. How uncertain are the traditions of the founders of the stupendous Pyramids & other wonders of Egypt. Where are the Registers of
100 Greek Temples in Sicily & how doe the Antiquarys perplex themselves in tracing the origin of most of the glorious Remains of Rome?
Therefore it behoves us whilst yet we have a glance of our own
country not inglorious Ruins

[54]

not idly to sit down contented with vulgar or learned opinions that
have no solid foundation but

[55]

endeavor to snatch them from the gaping jaws of irrecoverable
oblivion.

against Webb

Let us proceed in our description of Stonehenge. The great error of
our Editor consists principally in two things, in that he has perverted
the scheme of its internal Part the Cell, & then has converted it no
less than 60 degrees from its true position in regard to the heavens so

that a line drawn thro' his cell which should goe to the North east
entrance at the ditch & which he acknowledges; will fall 75 foot
distant from that entrance on one side, in his own scheme. His notion
of three entrances is but fancy grounded upon the equilateral triangles which he has drawn two remaining stones near the ditch out of
their true places to countenance. For them two stone by no means
form a triangle with the North east entrance. The truth is thus.
Round the great Work of the Temple is a great circular Area enclosd
by a ditch which he says is thirty foot wide, which we may well allow
to be [30 Celtic (9.2 m), deleted] it being thro' so vast a space of time
well nigh leveld. This ditch is continued quite round except at the
grand & onely entrance in the north east[73], & no doubt was intended
to keep out cattle as well as to give a great lustre to the Work &
secrete the consecrated ground. The earth thereof is thrown on the
inside, at first was sufficiently provided against in the declivity of the
whole spot towards the meridian sun. A Sett from the foot of the
outer circle of the Temple reaches to the middle of the ditch, so that
the interval of 80 (24.4 m) defines a circle concentric to the whole
work quite round the Area within the verge of the ditch.

[56]

The oval figure of the cell answers pretty much the sacred prophy-
lactic tables of the Egyptians which so oft occur in their hieroglyphic
carvings.

[57]

This Area enclosd with a ditch well setts off the temple & heightens
its majesty, there can be no difficulty in supposing its use was to
receive the vast concourse of the devout & to prepare the sacrifices in.
The whole work then reckoning the mound on the outside equal in
bredth to the ditch is precisely 400 feet (122 m) in diameter.[74]

[56]

The additions to Camden make 35 yards (32 m) from ditch to the
work 10. 20. 30. 40. makes 100.

[57]

Which tho' finall in comparison to Abury yet dos not deceive the
Founders intention in being a most illustrious & refind copy admirably
well calculated for its purpose & could not fail of giving the spectators

an infinite surprize & pleasure withall that saw it in perfection as even now in its ruins.

avenue

But there yet remains the Avenue to be spoken of, to compleat its glory. Just upon the Entrance into this Area lys a stone flat upon the ground of a large size,[75] there is left of it now $21\frac{1}{2}$ foot (6.6 m) in length & 7 inch bredth, so that it was equal to the upright stones of the Cell. From hence goes the Avenue extending its self to the length of 1700 cubits descending gently all the way to the bottom of the Hill,

[56]

tis in the Hebrew measure 1000 cubits, & with this view Stonehenge was set just where it is, that from the valley the just length of 1000 upon rising ground should reach it, for higher up the ground still rises beyond. 1000 cubits from the bottom to the cursus.

[57]

But first at the distance of 100 feet (30.5 m) from the circle of stones within side the ditch, stands a stone of a vast size rather bigger in base than any we have yet describd in this Work,[76] its position in respect of the middle line of the Avenue is the same with that of the portal before describd, answer it & both servd as those the same purpose, to constitute [another portal, deleted], but tis worthy remark that from the stone of the innermost portal which we mentiond to lye flat on the ground & from the two remaining stones of the circle enclosing the Area the Editor focuss his uncooth gates or entrances which have nothing Roman nor Celtic nor reality its self, for the stone marked E in his first plate[77] which he says is one of those great ones making the entrances from the outside of the trench & whose dimensions he gives

[59]

against Webb

exactly, dos not lye in the place he has assignd it without the ditich with its nearest end quite within the ditch, which is 37 foot (11.3 m) distant: but of the other two supposed entrances within the ditch of a lesser size marked E.

This stone in girt (of the outer portal) is $24\frac{1}{2}$ feet (7.5 m) $16\frac{1}{2}$ (5 m) high 6 thick 9 broad.

Between the middle of each ditch of the avenue is 75 Celtic feet (22.9 m).[78]

[59]

That on the right hand or West of the Temple by him is placd 64 foot (19.5 m) by his own scale distant westward from its real place, & that on the left hand or southern pretended entrance no less than 135 feet (41.2 m) too much southward along the verge of the ditch than is its present seat. So that in case this whole monument had chancd to have been destroyd since his time, & that the stones were not now upon the spot to prove my assertions, I leave the Reader to judg, how true a representation we should have had of Stonehenge, which truly, for the most part as there deliverd is formd ex ingenio, as he would have had it, to corroborate his hypothesis, not as it is, tho' thereby in my judgment it would have had no more real advantage, than the Romans of honor by being enlisted to its foundation, for as I think it wants not any Roman finery to bedeck it, so the Roman Architects were they calld from the dead, would absolutely disclaim any pretence to a structure of this sort, that is so extravagantly distant from their Rules & Ordonnances of Architecture, civil or sacred.

[58]

Area

85 feet (25.9 m) 50 cubits from the outside of Stonehenge are placd 2 stones one to the northwest the other leaning now to the east directly opposite to the other[79], they being upon the extremitys of the same diameter. 60 cubits from the outside of Stonehenge the inner verge of the ditch begins. Tis 20 cubits wide.

[59]

avenue

Of the other stone we mentiond standing in the avenue, the Editor makes no mention tho' it is of as great dimensions as any we have describd, nor is there the least notice taken of the avenue, tho' the two ditches that formd the outside of it are very visible the whole length. This upon my first journey hither, I discovered, answering to the entrance of the area & principal Entrance of the Temple. When Mr Roger Gale & I measurd it more than once. [There is not one stone left therof, yet a curious eye without difficulty will discern a mark of the holes whence they were taken tho' the ground, deleted[80]] is so much trod upon, & moreover the course of a horse race traverses it about the middle. This magnificent Walk or Entry is made by two [rows of stones containing fifty on a side so that in the whole they compleated the number that makes but one side of those at Abury, yet therein it cannot be denyd that this proportion fully answers the more contracted extent of the whole work, deleted], moreover this is gracd with a ditch on the outside, & is drawn perfectly strait from one end to the other, & perfectly adjusted to the temple its self nor dos it run over such unequal ground but you may nearly see from one end to the other, which were advantages scarce to be had or disregarded in the excessive magnitude

[61]

& extent of Abury. The manner of forming the Avenue is thus they took 40 cubits which is equal to three intervals of the circle of stones in the Area & therewith markd the distance between each stone lengthwise in 50 times 40 measures 2000 feet (610 m) on each side for the length of the avenue & 40 (12.2 m) the bredth all the way included between the two which stand in a square all along. & the two intercept of that circle about the Area the grand Entrance. The ditches that guard its outside are but a third of the bredth of the great ditch that encloses the work the earth too is thrown on the outside which being of equal bredth with the ditch, brings the whole bredth of the avenue, measuring to the extreme side of each bank to 100 feet (30.5 m), proportion being every where observd thro' every part & thro' the whole, & generally that of a third, thus besides the many we have observd all along the bredth of the opening of the cell included between its first pyramids is a third of the diameter of the whole Temple, & forms an equilateral triangle with the inside of the grand entrance at the outer circle of stones. Coinciding with the union of the two arks that close the two circles of the ellipsis in the cell. The same opening of the compasses marks the other point, & third part of the whole diameter upon which one side of the altar lyes. The diameter of the Temple is a third of the diameter of the great ditch that encloses it. Nor is the length of the avenue without an analogy to the whole work its diameter 400 (122 m) being a 5th. Thereof 2000 (610 m). If again we consider the number of the stones employd in this building we shall find a regular ratio observd in their distribution & in the whole. Particularly all the denarys [tens] included in half a hundred, we may thus reckon them up & which is a new argument & a strong one that we have not errd in the description.

first, the Altar stone _____ 01
the great architraves of the Cell _____ 05
the uprights of the Cell that support them _____ 10
the internal Pyramidal stones of the Cell _____ 20
The external Circle of uprights _____ 30
the architraves of the same circle _____ 30
the circle of pyramidal stones _____ 40
the circle that enclosed the Area _____ 02

Toto 140[81]

[60]
O N

75 feet (22.9 m) measures the bredth of the avenue from the middle of each ditch. 40 cubits British within from edg to edg. The reason of difference in the pyramidals is only to accommodate the who n°. of upright stones to 100.

That the patriarchal temples were like ours, of huge stones prepared from Jacob summoning all his family together. From Gideon in *Judges* VI. taking an oxen & 10 servants to throw down Baals altar so that what Gideon built remains to this day & they had an orderly manner or form as in v.26 & that form was round as we gather from οιχον Ων ['round dwelling'] calld the Suns temple because like his disc. So the Thracians made the like to Macrobius' *Saturnalia* I. 18. They calld the deity Sebadius. Macrobius would know it Apollo & Bacchus.[82] The learned Meursius will have it to Jupiter Sabazius *a como apallatio* in inscriptions. I suppose it was originally to *HΛ* the [supreme, deleted], from whence Idolatry made *Ηλιοs* [helius]. & this was favord by the round form of the temple & being open at top. I suppose much like ours. For we cant think they made a pantheon in Thrace. It was upon the hill Zilmissus. Thus Orpheus *Εις Ζεμs, εις Αδπs, εις Ηλιοs, εις*

ΔιovoCos ['Zeus, Adonis, Helius, Dionysus'] all one the 2^d. deity.
These are only strong approaches to verisimilitude. We have nothing
else left for it. & I see no reason to doubt it.

[62]

A stone as big as any at Stonehenge lys about 3 mile in the cornfield
directly from the work beyond the length of the avenue in in
Durington [Durrington] field & another in the Water at Milford,
another at Fighelden [Figheldean] which I suspect were carryed back
to make milldams or the like in the river. There is another in the
London road from Amsbury about a mile from the town so that one
would rather guess they were sett there for guides to the Britons when
they came hither.

The Messenians usd to tye a bull to a great stone when they sacrificd
to the famous Aristomenes & take augurys from the bulls fury &
resistance in shaking the stone. Pausanias' *Messenian* [Note 43. Book 4,
Messenia.]

[63]

Behold the solution of the mighty wonder of Stonehenge, the magical
spell is broke which has so long perplexed its admirers, & so much in
the mouth of the vulgar that they think nothing of so extraordinary
in it but an impossibility to number them.

[62]

So prevailing is superstition that the cant of counting these stones
immediately recurs, not only to the vulgar & ignorant, as soon as
mention is made of them.

[63]

That tis an ominous thing & great danger that people will dye after it.
Nor dos it seem less surprizing that Abury dos not exceed in a larger
proportion when it has two avenues of 200 stones each for that
reaches but to 750 in all. Thus in the whole doe these noble works
fully answer the definition I have in the beginning given of beauty, a
well varyd collection & regular system of proportions in finall
numbers. For view them every way, & collate their components what
manner you please, they are of one kindred & physiognomy & sym-

metry. Like as the operations of the Supreme Master of Architecture
from the lowest to the highest beauty. How many measures & equal
subdivisions doe the painters & statuarys find in the human face how
are they multiplyd & compounded to fetch out the secrets of his
Divine Art, & of the human body in general we need only to contem-
plate a little the admirable plate publishd by Martinez sufficient to
convince us of this great truth. I find that the avenue of Stoneheng
tho it consists but as that of Abury, bears likewise the same porpor-
tion to the Diameter of the Work for the circumference measurd in
the middle of its environing ditch, as we did before at Abury, is 1000
feet (305 m). Now after these strict resemblances, we must abandon all
logic, to doubt they had all the same founders, so that the number of
them & their diffusion thro' all the Brittanic Isles without the least
assistance of other argument, must be an unsurmountable bar to any
pretension of Roman Authors, & a conclusion more weighty than the
united bulk of the very stones. & the silence of Roman writers in this
affair is a stronger presumption on our side than against Us for it had
been an inexcusable neglect & defect in History not so much as to
have hinted at a thing so very extraordinary, they tell us of their
making great Roads here, of draining marshes of building citys,
Temples, Theatres, but had they been Authors of a new scheme of
Architecture of building in this manner so different from their former
& of so numerous specimens of the Brittanic order as we may call it,
the Emperors had just reason to perpetuate it by coyns, inscriptions &
all their glorious methods of immortality. & there had not been one of
these Temples without pompous memorials deep cut in this lasting
matter of their composition, how many *basso releivos*[83], altars, sacrificing vessels & instruments should we

[65]

have found about them, above or below ground, instead of which
there is no single instance of any such thing, & what harvest of coyns
ought have to be expected, at which they must have workd so long a
time, & much fragmented but nothing of this sort appears, & after all
the digging that has been at Stoneheng our Editor says only a small
cover of an earthen pot was discovered (p.76) which he supposes was
the cover of a *thuribulum* or some such like vase, to carry incense wine
or holy water for service in their sacrifices.[84]

[64]

But to talk of a Roman *thuribulum* cover is as unintelligible to me as
making Stonehenge Roman.

[65]

Had the Romans been the only people in the world that made
earthen ware or had this been truly Roman, there had been no occasion for supposition. If the signature of the Potter had been stampt on
it, or could the Author who doubtless had seen many Roman vessels,
have assurd himseld of its being their work, he was much too blame
not to give us a draught of it, for theres little difficulty in distinguishing theirs, & then at best nothing ought to have been concluded from
a single instance of a thing which proves its self but a casuality. &
where every other circumstance makes against him but not one to
back the supposition not so much as a casual coyn. Then how hard a
talk is it for any one to account for this unaccountable labor, utterly
abhorrent of Roman Politicks & usage, who ever mixd use & pomp
together, & never forgot above all things the sure & undoubted evidences of their presence in all their undertakings, that posterity
should have no room to doubt of what is truly their own. When was
it heard or suspected that the Romans built a Pile like Stonehenge at
all, much more in the midst of a vast solitary plain, distant from any
of their forts, towns or roads, for what use is it accommodated
according to their manners & customs of which we have the minutest
intelligence? Temples they built in citys or near them, garnishd with
Altars, statues, elevated on steps & adornd with the flower of Archi-
tectonic skill not the bare magnitude only of a few simple & natural
proportions, if its designd for a trophy of some great victory where
the fragments of Arms, ensigns, Citys, captives inscriptions cut in
stone statues? Barrows there be indeed & many but only a single
corpse found in each, were they so complaisant as to raise a tumulus
for every soldier of the enemys army? & if so their glory had not
merited a triumph in defeating such a handful of men, or if such
monuments were designd for a Captain of their own, they would have
little reason to have boasted of a victory, if Stoneheng had been a
Monument raised by them what is its signification, what means its distinction into circles & Area & to what purpose its long Avenue, where

are the Urns the Inscriptions of *Dis manibus* ['spirits of the dead'], the
medals & other matters the lacry-

[67]

matorys, the lamps & other funeral concomitants? But indeed tis time
to close this argument in a matter that to me seems unnecessary. Where
tediousness would be trifling, had it been an objection of my own
raising, & not shrowded under a name that I my self revere as much as
any man living for his greatest ability & most perfect understanding of
what is both Theory & practise of true Roman Architecture. & I would
sooner with the worst to my own memory, if any I deserve, than wilfully offend his Illustrious Shade, whose honesty, & love of Truth, &
sense of human error which all are lyable too, I doubt not, if it know
the sincerity of my intentions & the high value I have ever conceivd for
him, would be the first to rise & plead my excuse.

[64]

This year 1723. Mr Thomas Haward [Hayward] owner of Stonehenge
showd Lord Winchilsea & me a brass coyn found at Stonehenge tis a
Faustina the Reverse *veneri victrici* ['honour to the victors'] at bottom
SA.[85] He says he has dyg there but found nothing but heads of oxen
& other beasts bones. But in 1724. several little worthless Roman
coyns were found superficially there, even while I was at the place by
Richard Haynes. Mr Merril gave him half a crown for one. I conjecture some body lately threw 'em there, or he might himself for the
premium, save such from Haradon Hill for this purpose.

The stones or rocks on which Hercules as they fable built Tyre after
he had fixt them were calld *Ambrosiæ petræ* ['stones of Ambrosius'],
coyns of them. I suppose them some extraordinary great stones set up
for a temple like Stonehenge. Probably this work of Stoneheng in the
original was namd too Ambrosiæ relating in the old Punic to some
what of this sort of works, hence in antient times they wrested the
story & origin of Stonehenge to Aurelius Ambrosius, & stones of this
nature now in Cornwall are calld *Amber* & *main amber* & the like
words.[86] For main amber is in British ambrosiæ petræ. p.170.

Am signifys circum in composition. Perhaps it means circular works of
stones. Ambrosia signifys divine. & sweet oil, which was pourd

perhaps upon there altar stones, *lapis unctus betylus*.[87] What it means in Hebrew I know not.

Ambres probably the name of Stonehenge, Ambres bury is the camp by the Ambres whence the name of the town. Amber the gum perhaps from being part of the compositum of the incense usd here. *Ambra lat. barb.* the same as *succinu*.[88]

[66]
Four circles here as at Abury enclosd in one larger.

[67]
Of the Danes & Saxons being Authors of Stonehenge I have said somewhat already & but little is necessary for two reasons, first was there most substantial evidence on their side it will only lower the Antiquity of our Monument but not alter the title of this discourse for they were undoubtedly a Celtic people as well as the Britons & if they built this it would not infer they built all that we treat of for how many have we enumerated in places ever possest intirely by the antient Britons; but it appears to me an impossibility to prove or to show its likely that they built in stone at all before they came to be Christians, & what few remains we have of their antiquity they were notoriously different from any thing of this sort, their manner was to make little narrow slits for windows & turn low doors with many small stones & much mortar, into semicircular arches, which tis evident they learnt from the remains of Romans buildings then subsisting in the Island, stone roofs pointed & wide arches & lightsome windows were introduced a good while after the Norman Conquest. But 2[dly]. all this whole matter is sufficiently & copiously handled by Mr Webb in his vindication, & I would not steal from him a plume he has just pretence to. My real intention is to pursue latent Truth & strict justice which only inducd me to plead the cause of the Britons who with the Romans Saxons & Danes are but our Common Ancestors, not dos the united blood of all those brave People run idly in the veins of their not degenerate Posterity.

[69]
I hope from the foregoing lines & the draughts that accompany them somewhat is done to preserve these glorious ruins, & that we cannot much fail of gathering a pretty perfect Notion of their Original per-

fection which must unavoydably engage us into the sentiment of those that think they were Temples. All the parts & the whole nature of them demonstrate it & nothing else. Whatever has been dug up prove the same, Mr Camden says mens bones have been found hereabouts & Mr Webb says the heads of bulls or oxen of harts & other such beasts have been found buryed in & about it as divers then living could testify, undoubted reliques of their sacrifices, he adds great quantitys of charcole all which particulars we observed before of Abury, upon which he brings Plinys testimony to prove the Romans used charcole as if burnt wood when buryed in the ground by any people Was not true charcole. But eternally to be lamented is the loss of that Tablet of lead & tin mixed together which was found at this place in the time of Henry VIII. inscribd with many letters but in so strange a character that nether S^r. Thomas-Elliot a learned Antiquary nor Mr Lilly Master of S^t. Pauls School could make any thing out of it.[89] Now to suppose these were Phænician letters as dos Mr Sammes can easily be allowd of that the Tyrian should march up into the midland country to make such a building is probable as all the notions he advances in his whole book out of Bochart p. 495[90], but without all question this was the language & the work of some famous Druid that had a main hand in the bulky composure, & had it been preservd till now I doubt not but would have savd us the pains of this disquisition & sufficiently have evidencd the truth of our opinion. For tho' Cæsar tells us they wrote in Greek, yet its not to be supposd Greek words. But their language in characters like theirs, that is the old Ionian Alphabet which is the foundation of all others, as Pliny says VII. 57.

Gentium consensus tacitus primus . . .[91]
['The first of all tacit agreement between the nations was the convention to employ the alphabet of the Ionians']
Pliny, Natural History VII, lvii, 210.

In the chapter before he had said that the use of Assyrian letters had been from all Eternity which is information enough in his circumstances, of their eastern original & that they were [deleted] with mankind & dispersd thro' all nations upon Earth, some whereof possibly might become so stupid as to lose them.

[68]

& all in a good measure alterd the form of them as well as run in to different dialects of the original language. & its probable that what Cæsar says of our Britains using the Greek character in his time might be more exact than formerly when their trade & inter course with the Gauls might reduce it nearer that modern Greek by way of the Massilian Colony, & in Harry VIII time the learned were little versd in Celtic Antiquitys.

[69]

This account of this metal is like that I spoke of before from M^r. Aubrey of five pounds worth of pewter found near here at Norman-ton ditch, the antient manufacture & traffic of our Ancestors from earlyest times.

[68]

Deity patriarchal

D^r. Stillingfleet thinks Stonehenge dedicate to Markolis who Buxtorf says the Rabbis call *Domu Kolis* see the Talmud Lex. v. Markolis. Pausanias' *achaic* [Achaea^{92}], says the antient Greeks worshipt unhewn stones insted of idols, more particularly that near the statue of ♀ [Mercury] near the pharii were 30 square stones which they worshipd. This I suppose an antient patriarchal temple but in time turnd to idolatry.

[71]

against Webb

Under these discouragements & after the very gleamings of what memoirs might have given us light are lost We must apply the touch-stone of reason & let down the bucket of conjecture into the Well of truth, & dip into the sliding streams at the Rivers mouth before lost in the Ocean of oblivion. We have spoke already of circular forms being the most antient for temples, nor is it less probable that they were open at top that the Persians & the Germans were so accustomed we have express proofs & that the Greeks Romans & other Nations fre-quently practisd it is as evident. & in the first ages of Mankind when they could scarce build roofs for themselves theres less reason to suppose they did to their Temples. Especially before the extravagant pomp of fine statues & costly ornaments made it more necessary.

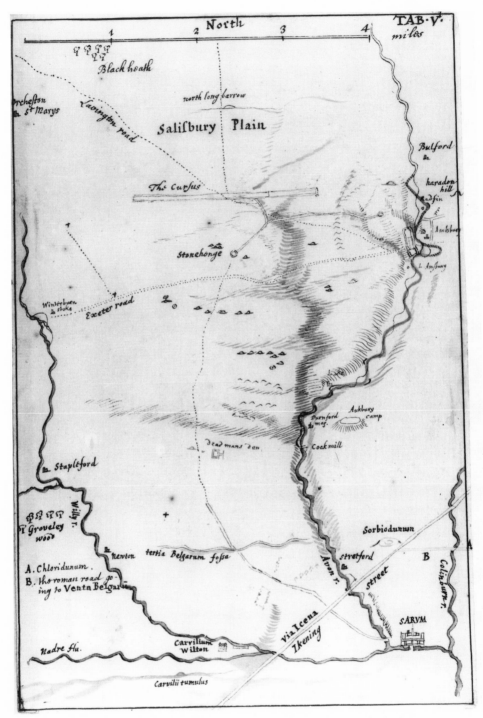

1. Stukeley's Sketch Plan of Salisbury Plain (Bodleian Library, Oxford).

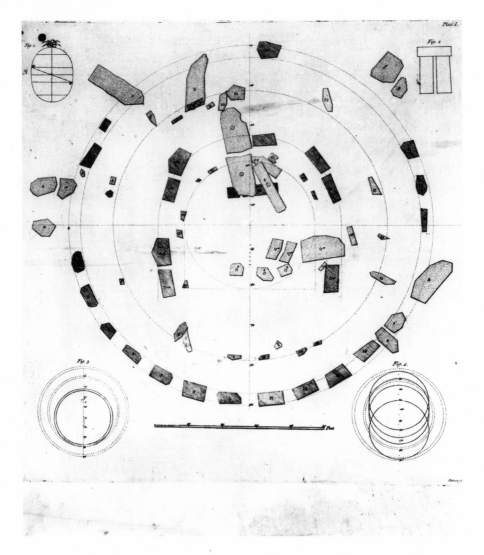

2. Stukeley's Plan of the ruined Stonehenge from the North East (Bodleian Library, Oxford).

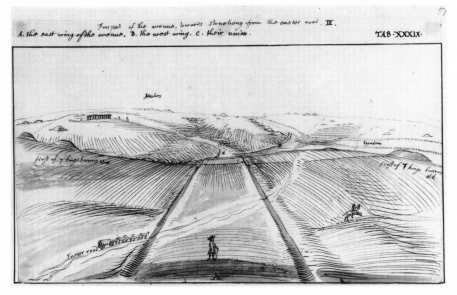

3. Stukeley's Sketch of the Avenue (Bodleian Library, Oxford).

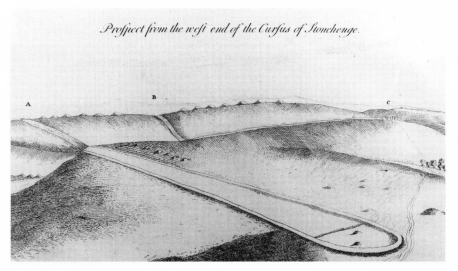

4. The Cursus, from *Stonehenge*, 1740

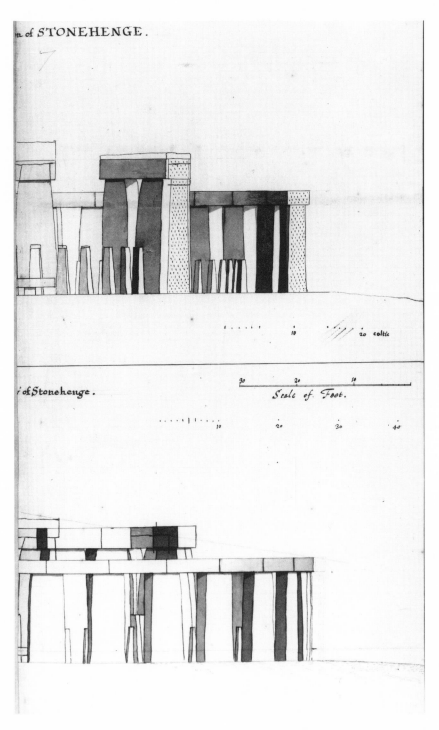

of Stonehenge.

Scale of Foot.

5. Stukeley's Sketch of Comparative Trilithon Heights (Bodleian Library, Oxford).

6. Stonehenge looking North East

7. Stonehenge from the South

8. An Ancient Briton, from *Stonehenge*, 1740

9. A British Druid, from *Stonehenge*, 1740

A British Druid

Stukeley designavit.

G. V. Gucht. Sculpsit.

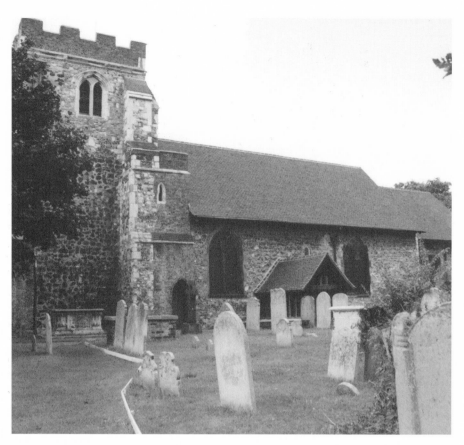

10. East Ham Church

Thes sort of temples were calld Hypethre & its to be hoped there is much better evidence than our Editor brings p. 77. to prove the Romans built such structures as Stonehenge from a quotation out of Varro which was no other than a birdcage. & as to his long argument following to prove the Monopteros kind of building had no roof, to what purpose is it when he owns p. 76. this temple is Dipteros & double wingd, moreover how is it compatible with our Antiquity when the Monopteros by Vitruvius is said to be without a Cell & tis manifest by his own confession all along that Stonehenge has one. & all that he says about Porticos being placd within such temples as were hypethre tis pure fancy when applyd to Stonehenge for as we said before the Pyramidals within the cell are double the number with the stones of the Cell & but a third part of their height but the notion is so crude as deserves no answer if supposd to be built by or in imitation of the Romans, & in relation to his disingenuity in a quotation out of Vitruvius thereto, III. & I refer the Reader to D\. Charlton. True it is the Romans never built Temples perfectly without roofs like ours but that was hypæthre which had an aperture in the top of the Tholus as now in the Pantheon, that of Romulus at the bottom of the Palatin hill. That most antient one near the *Via Sacra* of Romulus The Temple of Jupiter in the Tiberine Island dedicated to Æsculapius. The Temple of Hercules by the Tiber. The Temple of the Sun built by Aurelian & others. All which were derivd from the mode of antiquity, both in this respect & that they were round. Vitruvius prescribes to us I. 2. that we should make these kind of Temples to Jupiter the Thunderer, to heaven, the sun, & moon, becaus we see the appeareance & effect of these deitys in the open & broad light. As for those that had porticos within they were ever of a square form. In general it seems to me most likely that the square form of

[73]

Temples was first introducd when they began to cover them such being more commodious for roofing either in stonework or timber as first practisd in the temple of Solomon. The Greeks too had the same method for Pausanias' *Attica* I[93]. mentions the Oracle of Nox & the Temple of Jupiter Pulvereus having no roof. But still these I suppose nothing like ours as wholly wanting any sort of Roof wherefore Barbaro in his comments upon Vitruvius I. IIII. says the Thracians were the only people who made round temples open in the middle & without a roof as under this form hinting at the Suns disc. & as they were open & roofless, so they understood the sun to be superior to all things & that his light was every where diffusd. What could he say better to describe our Temples & who were the Thracians but the Ancestors of the old Britons? At Abury it would have been absolutely impossible to make a roof of any timber whatever & at Stonehenge no one can imagine there was any designd.[94]

[70]

We may well suppose the antient way of sacrificing here practisd like that in most antient heathen authors & that like as by the Jews, & that like as in patriarchal times. Therefore we shall subjoin from [incomplete]

Homer describes the manner of the Greeks sacrificing an hecatomb at Chryse, adequate to the method & model of our temple in *Iliad I*.[95]

> *lu auto stati deo inclyta hecatombe,*
> ['Straightway in haste, a chose hecatomb
> To God, prepar'd, the well-built altar round,
> They place in order. Then their hands they wash,
> And take the salted meal. Aloud the priest,
> With hands uplifted, for the assembly prays.
> After the prayers, they wav'd the salted meal,
> And then retiring slay the animals.
> The skins being stript, they cut off both the thighs,
> And cover them with cawl; first offer'd crude,
> The priest then burns a part on plates, thereon red wine,
> Libation pour'd. The ministring young men
> Stand by him, with their five-fold spits in hand.
> But when the thighs are burnt, out of the rest
> Entrails and flesh, harslets and stakes they make,
> Upon the spits transfixt. Then roasted well
> They set all forth. After the duty done;
> A feast they next prepare. Plenty of food
> Distributed around, chearful repast.

Banquet being o're, the youths huge goblets crown,
And fill to all in cups. Then sacred hymns
Sung to the Deity, conclude the day.

Homer, *Iliad, I,* 448–75.

V. Natal. Comes I. 10 explaining this whole matter. Homer describes
this again in *Iliad II.*[96] with some little variation thus see the Hebrew
rites.

[73]

August 4. 1723. I first discoverd that the Avenue of Stoneheng[97] went
farther than the bottom of the hill & turning with a sweep eastward
mounts the opposite hill at the end of the seven barrows. Both the
ditches continue 75 feet (22.9 m) asunder & 300 feet (91.4 m) beyond
where the 7 barrows[98] appear in a strait line it is sadly cut off by the
arable land which continues for a mile together as far as the River
side of Ambesbury. Tis so absolutely effacd by the plow that I could
not possibly discern the least traces of it, but it points to the River just
against the 7 barrows. East of Ambesbury in the London road,
between the bridge by the Abby & Rathfin farm, thither, no doubt it
was continud along a valley & up the next hill ore against the North
end of Vespasians Camp & probably terminated thereabouts being a
conspicuous place to all those that passd any of the fords in this part
of the River. However I measurd its extent as far as it was visible.[99] At
6 chains (120.7 m) beginning from the plowd ground the avenue is
opposite to the right line of the 7 barrows & the Eastern ditch is 257
feet (78.3 m) distant from the ditch of the nearest or most northern
barrow of the 7 & 350 (106.7 m) from the other ditch of the avenue to
the nearest of the six barrows, so that these two rows of barrows serve
as wings to it. The first plowd field, I learnt, was Mr Haywards (that
eastward) & the other of a different estate called Countess farm & the
plowing in these two goes contrary ways, beside I observd that arable
piece of Countess farm is long & narrow & perfectly by its whole
track & bredth demonstrates its self to have been really so much more
of the avenue which therefor I measurd 750 feet (229 m) in length. It
runs here 10 degrees South of East with the same obliquity as the
other parts.

[72]

Tis probable by the riverside at Bathfui & Ambsbury were Groves originally where the Britons first got the oak boughs & Missleto to adorn themselves & sacrifices in the procession.

It dos not appear that there ever were stones in this part of the avenue[100] & indeed one should not expect it because the strait part only would produce the effect, the other seems only to guide the procession by its ditches from some particular place where they all met & began it.

[75]

August 6. 1723. I discoverd the noble Ippodrom[101] of Stoneheng for nothing else can I suppose it, tis formd of two parallel lines 10000 feet (3048 m) 7000 cubits in length & 350 asunder going in a strait line from east to west, 200 North of Stoneheng. The vallum is inward of both (Plate 4). The eastern end is but a little eastward of the direct part of Stoneheng avenue where its terminated by a long bank reaching from one side to the other at the end of the 5 old barrows (without ditches[102]), almost answering the end of that strait part of the avenue & seeming the oldest upon the plain & are sett at a great but equal distance from one another. At the west end of this Ippodrom are two other banks going across which seem the starting places of the horses. Its general contriveance is to reach from the top of two gently rising hills descending both ways towards the middle, into a broad valley, which is at the end of the strait part of the avenue. So that the west end of the avenue turns with a sweep to the middle of the Ippodrom whilst the east is continued towards Ambesbury. This spot of ground for thes horses & chariot races declines a little all the way northwards for the most part of its length which appears admirably well contrivd for coolness & dryness & is an excellent descent & elevation from one valley up to each end, the whole extent, & within sight of Stoneheng but especially all along the next northern elevation. The northern group of barrows is drawn along its side at a convenient distance & their heights must afford a fine prospect of the races. & beyond it northwards are many barrows but very small, & seeming very antient, scatterd about here & there in groups & I observe generally in a row that runs East & West, but rather enclining to the south east. The eastern end of this Cursus inclines its level to the south & appears very plainly at Stonehenge & there are two entrances still visible thereabouts across each ditch almost answering the direct part of the avenue.

[74]
cursus Virgil Abury

Here I doubt not but Virgils beautiful description has appeard in full lustre. *Georgics III. Nonne vides cum precipiti certamine campum* ['Don't you see the chariot on the plain hunting in a torrent from the starting-gate'] &c. p.279. p.286. again p.905.[103]

A stadium says Pausanias in *Argolius*, at Epidaurus near the grove & temple of Diana made chiefly of earth.

Gyrfa cursus stadium British.

V. Diodorus p.303. of the cursus at Panchea.[104]

From west end of cursus to entrance of west wing of avenue 5350 feet (1630 m). From long meta Stonehenge is 236 (71.9 m). long meta[105] not a barrow because it has not proportion. An agreable group of barrows north of cursus. In the valley above the spring going to Shrawton [Shrewton] is a prodigious sight of barrows of incredible variety two druids[106] thus intrenchd upon one another. farther west-ward toward the mill a group with a druids thus. Each hollowd at top. See Drydens life of Plutarch.

I suppose the end of the avenue upon the hill North of Vespasians Camp northwest from Amsbury church. Here the horizon opens from Northwest to Southeast to the Avon so that you may see down the river nearly to New Sarum & upwards with all the hilltops east of Amsbury conspicuous for a great distance, it takes in a long scene of country considering tis not the highest ground hereabouts, but then tis near the river where their groves were, & has a fine gentle rise for half a mile & more. The hedges hereabouts towards the river are charm-ingly adornd with viorna[107]. & Avon is a delightful river flankd on both sides thick with villages & good land at the skirts of the downs.

Æneas praises the sybil as most usual & grateful
Tum Phebo & Triviae solido de marmore templa.

['In the marble temple of Phoebe and Diana justice is dispensed on festival days in the name of Phoebe']

Virgil, *Aeneid, VI.*

These were the ludi apollinares performd in the flaminian circus at the upper end of which was the ædes of Apollo whence some calld it the circus apollinaris. After sacrificing a bull adornd with trappings & gilt horns & two white goats with gilt horns, to the moon a black heafer with gilt horns says Pompou. Sabin. & this was the first & only temple of Apollo once in Rome. Pædian[108]. *in orat. contra Anton.* & *catalin.* Livy XL says there was a temple of Diana there. An altar of Neptune too as inventor of chariots & horses. Livy. Dec. 3. VIII. Pliny XXXVI.5 Marlian.

V.10. To Bacchus the *trieterica* [festival] every 3[d]. year.

[77]

Let us return by the Avenue the regular way to the Temple & there discourse further of what concerns our Antiquity, in order to apprehend rightly its grandeur & true purport we must first take a step in the East side of the River Avon a little above Amesbury, where on the brow of the bank we find seven barrows in a line by the road side which gives us an agreeable prospect towards the opening of the Avenue. For since its termination is plowd up & obliterated, we have no other means left to give a tolerable guess at the original nature of it, than a thorough consideration of the ground it passd over & the appeareance of the country thereabouts, & from that I don't much dispair of giving the reader some satisfaction towards recovery of this noble part of Stoneheng which an inquisitive person will be glad to be informd in. For tis not enough to project a stately structure & finish it without regard to our approaches to it, that highly recommend the principal part to us, & when well adjusted prepare in our minds a suitable Idea of the whole before we have seen it. & in this the founders of Stoneheng seem to have been very careful & have wisely pitchd upon the only ground hereabouts most commodious for their purpose. No doubt but the Inhabitants of the River Avon were mainly concerned in erecting this sacred structure as being but a mile & half from the side of the river, therefore these two points were had in special regard to make the entrance of the Avenue due East &

West[109], & to find the most easy passage to it, where the River is fordable for the largest space & where it is most conspicuous to the Inhabitants round about. It must then be noted that all along the western shore of the Avon, there runs the ridg of a hill & pretty high from a mile or two above Stoneheng quite to Lake which is as much below it, so that the Water falling upon the whole plain or that circular cavity wherein we said Stoneheng was scituate of three mile diameter all runs into the valley on the west side of this ridg stretching north & south into the River at Lake. Which no doubt takes its name from thence Leak or Loch signifying such a watery outfall & there are sluices.

[76]
Avenue

The Avenue to the templ of Minerva Cranea near Elatea is ascending but so gently that its inperceptibl. Pausanias' *Phoenix.*[110]

The grand entrance is the *Trias fontana horæa*, or *porta magna orientis* ['great eastern entrance'] opening to the Sun in its utmost exaltation in longest days. When he ripens all things. 5 degrees 43 from the east northward.

cursus

The Britons celebrated games every 4th. year, which they derivd from Hercules of Tyre. For they celebrated such at Tyre to him, & Antiochus Epiphanes king of Syria sent 3300 drachma to there, & at these ceremonys of the Druids they made their great sacrifice of malefactors. At the equinox or vernal solstice. From west end of cursus to the entrance of the west wing of the avenue is 5350 feet (1630 m) 3200 cubits.

[79]
Mr Hayward[111] deservs a greater encomium than my memoirs will afford for his love of Antiquitys & Zeal in preserving this the noblest of all the Britannic. Tis much to be wishd that it was securd not only from present but future ruin by some public sanction of the nation & likewise in time retrievd from what I fear a speedy deformity of some of its most considerable parts, for at the grand entrance where only 3 of the outer circle architraves are contiguous & which best at present gives an idea of its former state I observe there is good reason to

apprehend a speedy downfall if not prevented. Its probable some people have been digging thereabouts for treasure & loosend the foundation for the two uprights at the entrance are much declind outwards from their perpendicular & probably would have fallen but for the stay of the two outer architraves. Lord Winchilsea & I measurd their declension from the perpendicular & found em 2. foot 7 inches which with the original taper or retirement of the stones may well be reckoned 3 foot. & that is very considerable in 13 (3.96 m) high. The present upright[112] behind the high altar that is standing if so we may call it (a most beautiful stone) hangs over from the perpendicular no less than 9 feet 6. This would have met the earth long since but that one of the pyramidals within side luckily opposd its top to save it but people have discernd within memory that it recedes & is in utmost danger. But what is most to be lamented is the colony of rabbits adjacent which in my own observation have done prodigious damage & will in a little time infallibly ruin the whole if not destroyd. For they have undermind several of the stones very lately. & the whole compages of the cell next it northwards seems to have felt the violent effects of a languid & unheeded motion, outwards.

[78]
Cavitys

The circular cavitys are designd perhaps for the sacrifices that were offerd to the manes ['spirits of the dead'] for we learn from many passages in old authors that their custom was to perform this ceremony underground in pits & ditches. Thus Orpheus Argon antics describes the manner for Cizicus. Slain unawares by Hercules.[113] *regem undique circumfusi* . . . ['they completely surrounded the king'].

Hence in their conjurations where ghosts were to be calld up a ditch was always part of the ceremony. Orpheus in raising the furys to assist the Argonauts mentions this. He dug a threefold ditch & he pourd part of the sacrifice about the ditch. &c.

The Irish to this day use what is calld an Irish kettle in their armys march which is a great hole dug in the earth for dressing their meat.

The h[e]ather here planted by them. An herb which they had a great regard to.

[81]

Many of the barrows about Stonehenges as well as Abury & other like places have been opend from time to time, but tho' I have conversd with several of the people that did it, I could learn very little from them of any particularitys therein discoverable, especially what position the bodys found observd, in respect of the quarters of the heavens. In general they are sepulchral but these incurious enquirers regarded chiefly their expectation of finding treasure in them. My Lord Pembroke two year agoe sett upon this affair in earnest & with his usual exactness. He pitchd upon one of those barrows south of Stonehenge close upon the road thither from Wilton & on the east side of the road, tis one of the double barrows,[114] or where two are enclosd in one ditch, tis of a later make & a good bell fashion it bears from Stonehenge & the distance of [incomplete] feet on the west side of it he made a section from the bottom to the top quite thro, & from the center to one side of the circumference being an entire segment whence he found the manner of composition in the whole barrow, which is good earth quite thro' except a coat of chalk of about two foot thickness at top covering it quite over under the turf. Hence it appears that the method of making these barrows was to dig up the turf for a great space round till they had therewith brought the barrow to its intended bulk then with the chalk that is dug up out of the environing ditch they powderd it all over so that for a considerable time they must have lookd white till a swarth of grass is grown upon it & for some years after they might guess at the age of the barrow by that appeareance certainly our ancestors that made 'em had a great reverence & notion of sanctity in these domus eternales for bidding them so much as trampling on them which would have misfigurd 'em till they were throly setled & therefore at this day they are very regular & well defind. At the top or center of this barrow & not above 3 foot under the surface my Lord found the sceleton of the interrd in full & perfect form of a reasonable size. His head lying towards Stoneheng or northward. The bones were not much decayd.

[80]

There are more sorts of barrows at Stoneheng than Aubury, yet several sorts of barrows at Aubury not at Stonehenge, here are none at all set round with stones, because twas too far to bring them, or was it built soon after Wansdike? Here are no kistvaens.

Between Great Bedwin [Great Bedwyn] & Everley [Everleigh] some barrows, between that & Amsbury as you approach it by degrees they encrease prodigiously; dozens & scores lye together in groups all the way.

> *Matres atq[que] viri defunctaq[ue] coropra vita.*
> ['Women and men, and figures of great-souled heroes, their life now done, boys and girls unwed, and sons placed in the pyre before their fathers' eyes']
>
> Virgil, Georgics, IV, cdlxxv–vii.

The Manner of running round the funeral piles on horse back is extremely antient & questionless practisd here upon these level plains in the funeral rites of Patroclus *Iliad* I dn. XI [272–86] of Pallas.[115]

> *ter circu acsensos cricti fulygentis arnes* . . . ['three times the armed men circled the pyre']

A very nice account of the round temple among the Lyphboreans in Diodorus II. So among the Thracians.

[81]

Upon this My Lord designd to prosecute his enquirys by taking a barrow North of Stoneheng which would let him into the knowledg of what he proposd, & this is the nearest diametrically opposite

[83]

to the present & nearly equal distance from Stonehenge the contrary way. Here he made a cross cutt at top upon the points to Stonehenge & that at right angles with it but the violent rains that then happend hindered his proceedings.

[82]

The patriarchal manner of preparation when they set about building a temple is describd *Genesis* XXXV.2.

The medium circumference of the ditch 50 Celtic rods. Chloridunum bears Southeast from it. Upon the coggles lay great plenty of white wood ashes like a hearth much burnt wood intermixt like charcoal black & soft. This white was perfect pot ash & salt.

[83]

This year My Lord & I conferring upon this subject, he determined I should goe on with his work therefore by his order upon 27 August 1723. I begun with the last mentiond which he had made an entrance into. This is the outermost or that most easterly of the group of barrows north of Stonehenge & on the south side of the cursus. It bears [incomplete] from Stonehenge at the distance of 1910 Celtic feet (582 m) as we measurd it. When we had dug 6. feet we came to a great heap of coggles or flints gatherd from the surface of the downs & finding nothing under them we enlargd our cut to 10. feet diameter of a circle & found nothing at the depth of 10 feet upon which we left it, but remarkd that the composition was the same with that first opend by my Lord

[82]

being a yard thick of chalk quite about takin from the large ditch encompassing it. The 3 feet fat mold taken from the surface.

[83]

Then we went to the next adjoyning barrow[116] which is double being two inclosd in one circle & of the bell form the most easterly is less & lower. I conjectured this might probably be a man & his wife that were here buryd & that the lesser was the female & so it provd. After the turf was taken away by a cut we made from east to west we found the layer of chalk, then fine garden mold. About 3 feet below the surface we found a heap of coggles as before laid in a circular form humoring the convexity of the barrow this being about a foot thick lay upon a layer of soft mold another foot in which was enclosd an urn full of bones. This urn was of unbakd clay of a dark reddish color it was crumbled all to pieces. I savd a little piece or two of it, it had been rudely wrought with small mouldings round the verge & other circular channels on the outside & several indentures between made with a pointed tool as depicted in plate [incomplete] where I have drawn all the sorts of things found in this barrow. These bones had been burnt & were crouded all together in a little heap not so much as a hat would contain they were but small. The collar bone & one side of the under jaw are gravd in their true magnitude those & some of the teeth I carryd away but the first would scarce hold

together being very friable as were the whole having passd the fire.
Tis plain by their bulk that this must have been a girl of about 13 year
old but

[85]

we had fine amusement in picking up the trinkets & little utensils
found among the ashes which utterly dispeld our chagrin at the first
disappointment. These were beads of all sorts & in great number. Of
glass of diverse colors most yellow one black. Many single, many in
long pieces notchd between so as to resemble a string of beads &
these were generally of a blew color. Here were many of amber of all
shapes & sizes as flat squares, long squares, round, oblong, little &
great, many of earth likewise of different shapes magnitude & color,
some little & white, many large & flat like a button others like a pully
but all had holes to run a string thro', either thro their diameter or
sides, many of the button sort seemd to have been coverd with a thin
film of pure gold. These certainly were the young ladys ornaments &
had all undergone the fire so that what would easily consume fell to
peices for the most part, as soon as exposd to the air, the amber was
visibly burnt half thro' so that the outside fell off immediately twas of
the common yellow sort. But this person seems to have been an
heroin or Amazon for among the rest we found the head of her spear
as I suppose or a javelin made of brass flat broad & thin pointed at
top & sharp on both edges tapering narrower & thinner from the
shoulders at bottom are two holes where the pins run thro' to fasten it
to a slit made on the top of a pike. Besides there was a sharp bodkin
or such like thing of brass round, but at one end squard a little where
I suppose it was stuck into a haft. The reader may if he pleases fancy
it to be her needle or a pin to fasten on her mantle or some garment.
I still preserve what is solid & lasting but many parts of the very spear
fell away upon touching & many of the trinkets scarce lasted till I
had time to draw them out upon opening the papers at my Lord
Pembrokes.

[84]

In the *Philosophical Transactions* volume 185. p.221. is a curious account
of a very antient Celtic sepulture wherein these things are observable.
1. The bodys lay north & south but the heads to the south. 2. Many

sharp instruments of flint & hard stones were found under their heads with holes in them to fasten 'em to bits of stags horn & the like & several things like beads & button moles with holes drilld thro' em. 3 Several little urns with ashes. 4 Much ashes coals & burnt bones in the ground all about them which shows the people both burnt & buryd their dead, most of which particulars are common with ours here. 29. December 1724. Mr Sa[l]. Lethieullier[117] brought a broad piece of thin gold found lately near Baltimore in Ireland like that drawn out in Gibsons *Camden* discoverd by the songe of an old bard.

templum juxta jacet mulier bene cincta ['the temple by which lies a richly dressed woman from the blessed isle']

Scheffer wrote a piece *de orbibus tribus aureis* . . . ['a circular article of gold lately found in Scandia'] Mr Bridges has it. They were 3 pieces of gold as broad as a crown piece a rude head on them all, & a dog underneath with some flowerwork. He says bits of swords & spears & the like are frequently found in tumuli there & because they are so rusty that they can scarce be taken up. Printed at Holm. 1695.

Nicholas Keder in his discourse upon a British coyn p.73. says in Sweden they often dig up gold bulle or buttons like ours, & rings, armilla fibula & like trinkets of all sorts of metal.

[85]
After begging an excuse of the Illustrious defunct for my boldness & theft we recomposd her ashes & coverd them up as before but left visible marks of our work on the top of the barrow to dissuade any future enquirer again to disturb her & which was our practise in all the following.

[87]
I judg the reader with me upon reflexion will make no difficulty to beleive this was the Corpse of an antient Briton. The rudeness & simplicity of every thing therein sufficiently shows it, & that before the times of the Romans. & this evidences that they had the manner of burning the dead & probably the Romans & Greeks learnt it from the more antient & perhaps Celtic nations. For we have innumerable instances of all the inhabitants of the great northern Continent practicing it to say nothing of the people of America.

But this gave us no satisfaction yet as to the query which way the bodys were laid. So we proceeded to open the next barrow to it & enclosd in the same ditch.[118] At 14 inches deep the mold being mixd with chalk we came to the scull of a man & all the vertebræ of the neck so we tracd the body & laid it entirely open. Tho' this barrow was of that sort we suppose of the latest manner or bell fashion as thos near it yet all the bones were exceeding crumbly. The scull fell into many peices & the rest. It was the sceleton of a young man. The leg was a foot & at inch long all the apophyses fell off with a touch & the whole was perfectly rotten. His head lay northward, his feet rather to Stonehenge then directly south, which seems not designd.

[86]
Urn burial

Cæsars says expressly of the Gauls that they burnt every thing most valuable with the dead. Keysler p.112.[119] mentions a great number of Authors who had wrote of the urns found under tumuli in great quantitys in all parts of Germany. Cæsar says the funerals of the Gauls were sumptuous & magnificent see Ioscelius comment on that passage.

Livy speaking of the Gauls beseiging Rome says they burnt their dead in great piles, which place for ever after became famous & calld the Gallic burning place. So Tacitus of the Germans says that the bodys of famous men were burnt with certain sort of wood & that they threw in their Arms & sometime a horse into the funeral pile to honor the dead. They made their tombs of turf thinking great & lofty monuments lay heavy on the dead.

Strabo says all the Celtic nation (Gauls) were lovers of finery weareing golden wreaths about their necks bracelets upon their hands & arms, & the nobility had garments embroiderd with gold.

Pomp. Mela[120] confirms their burning 2.3. when they burn their dead they bury with them the account of their affairs & debts which may be carryd with them in to another state. & several have thrown them selves into the funeral pile that they might live with them hereafter. So Diodorus V. says they threw in letters to the flames that might be carryd to their friends & familiars. Valerius II.6.[121] speaks of the Mas-silian Celts the bodys are carryd to the place of sepulture in a waggon without any grief or mourning, the funeral is ended by a domestic sacrifice & a feast of the relations. For what dos it signify to indulge human grief or envy the divine being which would have us share with him in his immortality?

Diodorus in his [Book] V. speaking of the Gauls says both men & women wear golden ornaments such as bracelets about their arms & thick torques of pure gold about their necks & fine rings & likewise golden breast plates. Rubruquis says the Tartars burn their dead & preserve their ashes putting them upon high pyramids. Heraclitus says Servius *An*. II. thinking all things came from fire, bodys ought to be burnt as restoring its own.[122] V. v. volume *Philosophical Transactions* p.97.

[87]

Thus have we two instances of the positure of the bodys north & south with the feet southward. & in this which is a double barrow & doubtless made at the same æra the one is burnt the other buryd whole. My next purpose was to search into some on the other points of the compass in respect of Stoneheng. Therefore I went to a group of barrows westward whence Stonehenge bears east north east the barrow Lord Pembroke opend a little south of southeast the first I opened 15 degrees north of northeast. Here is a large barrow ditchd about but of an antient make on that side next Stonehenge are 10 lesser very small & as it were crouded together, south of the great one is another barrow but not equalling it in bulk. It should seem that a man & his wife are buryd in the two great ones & these little ones are their children. I cutt into one of the small ones[123] tho' 40 feet (12.2 m) in diameter at top we found a pretty formd flint of a coralline texture. 3 feet deep we found much wood ashes soft & black as ink we sunk a pit 9 foot diameter to the surface of the chalk natural. We

[89]

found a bit of the same kind of urn we spake of before of black & red earth very rotten, one little piece of human bone, some small lumps of earth red as vermilion, some flints burnt thro'. More burnt bones, vast quantity of light ashes as last upon the solid chalk in the center of the barrow was a little hole cut, it seems as if this was a childs body burnt on the spot & then coverd up. I counted from the top of the adjacent barrow 128 barrows in sight at once.

Going from hence more southerly there is a cavity by a great barrow the last of the Southwest group & Between it & what I call the Bush Barrow by the country people the Green Barrow. This is 100 Celtic feet (30.5 m) in diameter & about 7 deep in the middle tis formd very regularly like a dish & perfectly circular, the earth taken out of it seems to have been carryd to the neighboring barrow tis full of the pretty shrub calld erica with a blew flower heath, which was at this time in bloom. The sun beams striking strongly into this large bason exhald the sweetest smell imaginable much like a honey comb & very strong. It bears 10 degrees West of Southwest of Stonehenge. We made a cross cut in its center 10 feet every way upon the cardinal points of the compass. It's a very red garden mold with some flints in it no doubt but this is owing to the rains & dews & soil of sheep sheltering themselves in it thro so long a tract of time. We found a bit of red earthen pot thin & crumbly about a foot deep.[124] We dug two foot deep every way & found it plain earth that seemd never to have movd. Mr Duke of Lake[125] that was with us, says he never heard of any sort of coyn found in the many barrows dug up in this plain. He dug up a barrow once & found a body at the surface coverd with flints but he remembers not which way it lay. They found in a barrow between Woodford & Lake a scull so large that it was kept in Wilford Church upon the bier for many years as a sight. He says at 11 barrows (or the Prophets Barrows) they have plowd up frequently bits of urns & burnt bones.

[88]

The *Dii manes . . . Dii boni* ['divine ghosts . . . good spirits'] for main anciently signifyd bonus. Baxts horace p.9.[126]

In this childs barrow some round small flints like the boys marbles Cicero II.22 de leg. thinks burying the most antient & natural way as then the body is wrapd up in its mothers covering. Thus Numa was buryd near the altars of the fountain. The little tumuli were calld suggraudria, their bodys being so small make no tumor. Sextus philosoph. III says the Troglodytes cover the dead bodys by throwing stones upon them. S^t. Jerom says antiently they had the custom of putting gold & ornaments both of men & women into sepulchres. No doubt but this was for distinction of personages. The Augurs & priests markd out the ground for sepulture as sanctifying it.

Cicero, *Philipp. ix* [*Philippics:* see, Quintilian, *VII, xviii; IX, iii; vi.*] quintilian decl. the *domus exilis* Plutonia speaks of a sepulchre violated *sacratos morte lapides etian cineros & ossa religiose quiescentes fracta sparsiffet urna.*[127]

I saw some years agoe many brass bits of bridles rings glass & amber beads &c found in an old British sepulchre in a quarry near Blankney Lincolnshire then in the possession of Roger Widdrington Esqr. now Mr Southcotes, there were large bodys found along with 'em.

Pausanias best says the rogus [funeral pyre] of the sons of Amphion are half a stadium distant from their sepulchre (that is half a quarter of a mile) & in the *rogus* some of the ashes remain.

[89]

Next we dug up a Druids barrow[128] (as I call them) next west to Bush Barrow, Stonehenge bears hence 10 degrees north of northeast we made a cross section in the apex of the little tumulus in its center 10 feet each way a yard broad on the cardinal points. We found a hole in the center cutt into the solid chalk squarish 3 feet 8 long 2. feet broad pointing to Stonehenge directly different from North & South tis 2 feet 4. deep from the surface the artificial mold is not above a foot. In this hole we found

[91]

all the burnt bones of a man, but no signs of an urn. The bank on the outside the circular ditch that encloses this space of ground is 2 Celtic rods (10.1 m) broad (10 feet each) the ditch one, 12 (3.7 m) more in diameter within.

Next we dug up a long barrow by the road side from Wilton to Stonehenge, it is between south & southwest of Stonehenge, a druids barrow between it & that Lord Pembroke first opend. Tis but a small one 60 (18.3 m) Celtic feet long 30 (9.1 m) broad it points nearly to Stonehenge, we made at the north end a long cutt 28 feet (8.5 m) north & south five foot broad we dug to the solid chalk & found nothing. Then we opend the Druids barrow adjoyning which is 200 Celtic feet (61 m) diameter from outside to outside Mr Roger Gale Mr John Toll & Capt. William Herbert present & found a burnt body in a hole in the chalk as before.

After this I opend the barrow next that Lord Pembroke first cutt (adjoyning to the last) & enclosd in the same ditch.[129]

[90]

First we made a ['hole' or 'cut'] 12 feet (3.7 m) long 5 broad pointing to Stonehenge. It was composd of flints & chalk at top we found great numbers of frogs bones 2 feet $\frac{1}{2}$ deep. A very fat black earth all the way. 4 feet $\frac{1}{2}$ frogs bones in great plenty we dug 6 feet deep & finding no alteration from the black mold. there were snail shells too & frogs bones at the very bottom. Yet no sign of holes.

[91]

I orderd the pitt to be enlargd to 14 feet (4.3 m) square & 14 deep & to be sunk to the very bottom but nothing but several layers of dry flints very large. At the bottom upon the chalk I laid 3 half pence one of King Charles King William & King George & enclosd it with flints, so filld it up again.

Then I opend one of three little barrows[130] upon a declivity at the bottom of that hill where the Kings Barrow stands as vulgarly calld & by some Ambrosius's Barrow this is southeast from Stonehenge & across the deep valley that runs from Stonehenge into the River by Lake, but found

[90]

at 5 feet deep upon the solid chalk burnt human bones in a small compass.

[91]

From hence we went to the 5th. of the 7 barrows[131] or Kings Barrows south of the grand entrance or avenue & full east from Stonehenge vizt the 5th. from the avenue or most northern. Mr Roger Gale present. We found a large course of flints at the very top afterwards several bones great & small seeming to be of oxen, dogs &c. But broken & scatterd, with many evident marks of burning, then more fragments of great & small bones. The stratum of flints was a good yard deep & lay conformable to the external curve of the barrow. Under this was good earth. We dug about 6 feet deep & found nothing more.

I opend another great & very old flat barrow westward from Stonehenge.[132] 3. September by making a cross section in it (near the little one which I supposd a childs barrow) according to the 4 cardinal points. It was

[93]
barrows

good mold at top. Just under the surface we found many bits of bones of some quadruped an horse or ox or deer & a small sharp tooth like that of a dog or boar. They were broke in pieces & probably had been burnt. We found too several bits of a blue hard kind of marble like the altar at Stonehenge, some bits of small ribs. Then we came to ashes two feet deep. Thes bones which we found still were either burnt or broke to pieces. & lay scatterd all about in bits. We found some small long bones as of a fowl. Hens or the like & still much ashes. Even the chalk was burnt yellow so that the funeral pile was on the spot. Some bits of burnt pottersware. At 3 foot deep bits of bones. They are very hard & solid, more bits of a red marble. A small circular tooth like that of a rabbit or hare, a bit of bone we judgd human (One of my Diggers was Sexton of Amsbury). A bit of the leg bone of a man. The pinion bone of a goose or turkey, another long dog tooth a thighbone of a frog. A snail shell. We dug 4 feet deep & still finding scatterd bones without expectation of meeting any thing separate, we filld it up again.

My Lord Pembroke tells me there was a brass sword found not long since in a barrow dug up here & that it was sent to Oxford.

Of the Druids barrows all the earth of the ditch is thrown outwards. East of Bush Barrow is one where half the earth is thrown out & half in to make a barrow n°. [incomplete] plate. here is but one long oval or pear form barrow the first & biggest of the 7 beyond or east of the river.

At Ambrosius Barrow[133] as vulgarly calld the head of a spear of 20 weight was found or rather a poleax given to Colonel Windham as said. Mr Holland dug up 3 large barrows in Winterburn [Winterbourne] Stoke field to the bottom, found nothing there but 18 inches under the surface single bodys. In one the bones exceedingly large & a hole struck quite thro' the scull.

Mr Stallard gave the brass Celt found at a long barrow to Lord Burlington for Sir A. Fountain. Twas 13 inches long.

In digging the barrow east of Amsbury to make an alehouse of it they found all the bones of an horse.

[92]
beads

Mr Lwyd[134] gives account of some made of opaque or marbl chrystal *Philosophical Transactions* V. p.118. Some ombriæ found in a barrow ibid. p.121. He says the druid beads are generally glass &c. Amber beads with a brass kettle & a small millstone found in a morass Dr. Leighs Lancr. p.59.

At Waldersheal house Sir Robert Furnace's between Sandwich & Dover they dug away a great barrow 1725[135]. & found many British beads & some button molds cover'd with gold as we did.

[95]
Tumuli

The Thracians when their great men dye after 3 days they sacrifice in vast abundance & feast after weeping ore the dead body they burn it or bury it in the ground heaping a tumulus over it Herod. Terps. V. Here is an express testimony of an antient people akin to our Celts both burning & burying as we find on Salisbury Plain, & in fact the great plains in Thrace are now full of such like barrows as ours. & all the countrys of the antient Titans. Pausanias *thiar. vi*[136] says among the Hebrews & Pergamens the tombs of the silem to be seen whence he concludes 'em mortal no doubt but they were Titans.

I found this to be generally the geometry of the best turnd & latest barrows here.

Strike a semicircle between two parallel lines, with the same radius, turn an arck the contrary way on both sides ab. cd. touching the semicircle & the groundline, the points a d are the diameter of the barrow generally 100 Celtic feet (30.5 m). So that this barrow is comprehended between 4 arks each the 6th. part of a circumference. ab is = to b e, & that to fg or gh, or hi. From the verge of the barrow sett off 15 feet (4.6 m) each way ak, dl. Take 10 for the bredth of the ditch & 5 remains of the solid surface round the bottom of the barrow thus the whole diameter is 130 feet (39.6 m) the perpendicular altitude very near 30 (9.1 m).

Tacitus says of the Germans

sepulchru cespeserigit monumentoru[137] . . . ['In burial there is no ostentation . . .'].

Tacitus, *Germania, XXVII.*

our Bri[t]ons practisd the same therefore laid the bodys at the top that the earth might lye light over them. *niote subaerio qui nime . . .* ['open to the sky', Quintilian, *VI, ii.*] More of the form of burial there. *estatuent tumulu & tumulo selmnia mittent. æternuq locus Palunun nomen habebit* – VI. Many tumuli in the Orcades.

[94]
Cavitys

I conceipt that the cavitys in the plain of Stonehenge were to make their fires in & hang the kettles for boyling the flesh of the sacrifices in their anniversary feasts in memory of the dead. Such was the custom of the northern people & the people sat round here eating & drinking ale & making merry. Many accounts of it in their writers. They likewise drank healthy in their bowls to the memory of the dead buryed in the tumuli. As Snorro[138] shows us at large. V Alexand. ab alexand. V.22.

The peopl of Memphis says Diodorus Sic. I.51. think the space of life very short, therefor much esteem the celebrity of a name got by vertue [virtue] after death, calling the houses of the living Tuns because we inhabit them but for a small time, but the sepulchres of the dead they call eternal houses becaus there we remain for ever.

Their method here was to turn the patera upside down *vergere invergere* the Latins calld it, to sacrifice otherwise or *libare* was *supina planu.* See Servi. 1015. *Vergere intem est conversa.*[139] Hence the reason we find so many pateras in the tumuli of the Romans.

quator lic prinuma virgrantes . . . This shows the sanctity of tombs for none durst take away the arms & other trinkets they left there.

The sacrifices to the Manes I suppose were of two sorts thos publick performed in the month of February which by Numa was orderd only to consist of an even number of days & the private such as every one made for his friend.

A deep cavity circular by the most northern of old 7 King Barrows near the eastern end of cursus.

[97]

Avenues

There was a temple of Jupiter Labrandenus at Labranda a village
near Mylasa a city of Caria much frequented. The way leading
thither was calld sacred pavd 60 furlongs thro' which their processions
went in pompous solemnity. Philostratus[140] says you went to the
temple of Diana at Ephesus by a stone portico of a stadium. Strabo
XVII says the magnificent temple of Heliopolis had a pavd entrance
the bredth of one acre & length of 4 (oval) it was calld dromos or the
cursus & stony sphinges were placd about it. A great pavd way leads
to the oracle at Delphos. X.

Our avenue betw. the twice 7 King Barrow is contriv'd to pass over
the lowest ground for ease. Stonehenge strait avenue from the gate to
the valley is 1400 cubits, just twice the diameter of Abury. Tis 2000
feet 73 (634 m) bredth of avenue fro middle of each ditch.

The bowing stone *Kro Lechen*, perhaps the place of bowing adoration upon approach. It leans a hole in it as in that at Western Isles, at
Abury they say the devil threw it at the builders. They don't say the
devil built this place as comonly of stupendous. A sign tis a temple. At
the flat stone probably the place of lustration.[141] Or it was another
bowing stone the 2^d act of devotion, some what more shapely because
within the ditch. Dashing 10th. ivat. Then they went round the temple
in procession with the oxen.

from union of the 2 avenues the east wing reaches at 2700 (823 m) to
the Kings. 750 more reaches to the corn 300 . . . . .   750 (229 m)
to the bottom of the valley . . . .   2400 (732 m)
to the ridg of Vespasians hill . . . .   200 (61 m)
                                                            ───────────────
                                                              6050 (1844 m)
                                                               450 (137 m)
                                                            ───────────────
                                                              5600 (1707 m)

[96]

Urns

6 golden sepulchral urns in the King of Denmarks repository *Philosophical Transactions* V. p.131. found in the island of Fuenon. 1685. had
ashes. &c. another of chrystal.

ossaque lecta cado texit Corynaeus aëno
['and Corynaeus, gathering the bones, hid them in a brazen urn']
Virgil, *Aeneid VI, ccxxix.*

These urns of ours are made in a wheel Ephorus says Anacharsis the Scythian invented tinder, a double anchor & the potters wheel. Who was of the country whence our Ancestors came.

We have autority [authority] sufficient that burning the bodys of the dead was in use before the Trojan wars. *Iliad* Homer v.79. Hector says

Corpus anteno mea domum . . .
['but he must let them bring my body home so that the Trojans and their women can cremate it in the proper manner']
Homer, *Iliad, VII,* 79–81.

I doubt not but tis originally a Titan custom or Celtic because its so much spread. Whether it arose from the notion of fire purging all things & restoring them to to their original perfection. Euripides says the body of Clytemnestra was purifyd by that about. Other think tis with the purpose of reuniting the most subtle part in man to his principle which is fire. As Enstath says *Iliad* A. or that fire being a deity they had a mind to be [unknown] by it. As Clemens of Alexandria Protrept says. Some think it owing to the notion of Heraclitus holding fire to be the principl of all things, from which came all things & into which they are to be resolvd again. Servius *Ænid. XI.* Tertullian *ad martyr*[142]. Who say that Heraclitus threw himself into the fire to make experiment of his own doctrin. Tis certain the eastern part of the world the Indians always did it & some doe to this day which shows that it was usd soon after the flood before nations dispersd & perhaps it might be out of a detestation of the watry element & a remembrance of the flood for they had the utmost aversion of dying by water or being left there when dead. No doubt one reason is the change of people & governments & fortune of war that the tombs & bodys of the deceasd should not be misusd. Or from a conceit of noisom smells arising from the buryd bodys.

Cæsar VI speaks of the Gauls burning bodies as the Greeks & Romans. Livy speaking of the Gauls beseiging Rome (5.III.dec.) that they shew the slain of an heap & burnt them, whence the place became famous afterward by the name of the Gaulish busts. Tacitus speaks of the Germans burning.[143]

Mr Collins collector of the Excise informs me of many Celtic barrows in the Isle of Wight, which when opend had urns in them. Atheneus speaks of a very great tumulus in the isle of [incomplete].

[99]
Enginry
Some have thought nothing but Roman Machinery could have raisd thes imaginary architraves, but then it must have been since the seige of Syracuse when the Romans were so frighted when Archimedes put but a pole out thro' a port-hole.

sed tamen alterius facilis labor [but however easy the effort], Virgil g.t. Mr Keyster says 150 soldiers at a time have tryd to lift off some of the monumental stones at Dreut[144] in Germany but could not.

Alexander Necham[145] says of Stoneheng

> *Nobilis est lapidum structura chorea Gigantum*
> [The Giants Dance, a famous stone-worke stands
> Art did her best in bringing it to pass,
> Vaine prating fame, reports by Merlins hand
> In manner strange this work effected was]
> W. Camden, *Britain*, 1637, 253.

Tis not to be doubted that some sort of mechanical knowledg must have been in use from the beginning of nature & if mankind learnt nothing of this sort by tradition from the Antidiluvians yet they would naturally & of themselves soon find out the leaver especially, the very breaking a stick would teach it them, when we put it against our knee as a hypomochilion & pull it at both ends, & were impossible but that its power in lifting a weight must very soon be found out, then they had nothing to doe but multiply & magnify them to overcome any given resistance. But we find from history that in a very little while after the flood mankind exerted its self in an extraordinary manner as risen from a new birth they projected works of amazing magnificence, the tower of Babylon what ever it was, was a thing vastly great & shows they had workmen so early capabl of the most magnificent undertaking, & when Semiramis hewd a stone obelisc 152 feet (46.4 m)

long 24 (7.3 m) square out of the mountains of Armenia & set it up at
Babylon as Diodorus says is it to be doubted that they were great
masters in Mechanics, the like must be said of the Egyptians who
very early erected their pyramids, obeliscs, statues pillars &c all make
of stones of dimensions exceedingly great, & I suppose the authors of
our works here learnt their arts from the same spring as the Egyptians
did, Hermes Trismegistus.

Hence it appears the antients not only had a very good knowledg
of the mechanical powers, but the ambition of doing thes great works
prompting them studyd every day to find out more & improve them &
perhaps they were not behind hand with us, tho' afterward lost & the
very works themselves show it, *credite opibus* ['the works prove']. Some
will say perhaps they did it by an excessive number of men, but I
cannot grant it, suppose we apply 50 men to one of the stones at
Abury. Which is as many as can possibly stand round it without hindring one another, they could doe little or nothing toward raising it &
setting it into its place but they certainly usd engines of some sort or
other ingeniously contrivd to lift 'em up & let em down at pleasure as
is plain from the little stones put under them.

[98]
funeral games

Thus at the burial of Cyzicus slain unawares by Hercules in the
Argonautic expedition Orphius gives us an account of the games
performd after the funeral celebrity.

> *Ipse vero Aesonides opposuit orbus praemiu . . .*[146]
> ['in accordance with custom, they conducted funeral games on the
> Leimonium Plain . . . ']

Apollonius of Rhodes, Argonautica, I.

[100]
burning

So far were the Romans from teaching the Britons to burn dead
bodys says Mr Ainsworth in his learned commentary on Kemps antiq.
that they see even not to have learnt it from the Gauls but the Gauls
from them nor is it so much to be wonderd at when Pliny says our
Druids seem to have taught the very Persians I. The truth is it was an

eastern custom whence the Britons were a colony after the continent was peopled & learning advancd. Their manner was certainly the same as the most antient Greeks. They threw oxen & sheep into the pyre as Homer speaks. & as Cæsar says of the Gauls. Thus in Goodmansfields[147] Anno 16 [incomplete] they dug up many British urns of rude work unbakd always heaps of bones near. & so I found frequently in Wiltshire.

The very great difficulty which the learned make about gathering the bones distinct from thos of animals &c seems best solvd by supposing they had an earthen or an iron bier to burn em in or a coffin of wood tingd with alum as Ælian speaks in two places. So Cæsar. D[r]. Hubbard has some of it.

[101]

Though sepulchres may have given the first occasion to temples & it may often be hard to distinguish one from another yet I think the case is clear enough as to Stonehenge, tis not a monumental structure but purely a temple, every part, of its form its appertenances its manner its altar its adytum its area its avenue & the whole demonstrate it. Some of the stones in Dreut are calld le Drouwen Keysler p.102.[148]

Et nunc honos sedem tuus ossaq nomen ['now with honour give your bones']. Haradon hill.

Often when I have been in Stonehenge have I been rapt up in Jacobs soliloquy, how dreadful is this place this is none other but the house of God & this is the gate of heaven.

[102]

To demonstrate the truth of my Cubit measure by the most pregnant & incontestable proof I shall present the reader with a Catalogue of some of the measures.[149]

Interval between trilithons & inner pyramidals	1 Cubit
Interval between the uprights of the trilithons	1
height of the imposts of the outer circle	$1\frac{1}{2}$
bredth of the stones of the inner ellipsis	$1\frac{1}{2}$
heigth of the imposts of the trilithons	2
intervals of the outer circle	2
bredth of the grand entrance	$2\frac{1}{2}$
Entrance between outer pyramidals	$2\frac{1}{2}$

bredth of the altar 3
bredth of the stones of the inner pyramidals . . . . $1\frac{1}{2}$
bredth of the imposts of the trilithons 3
bredth of the jambs of the inner circle . . . . $2\frac{1}{2}$
central distance of the stones of the lesser circle . . . . . . $3\frac{1}{2}$
bredth of the uprights of the outer circle 4
interval between the inner & outer circle 5
mean heigth of the inner ellipsis 7
bredth of the uprights of the trilithons . . . . $4\frac{1}{2}$
between the outer wing of the cell & the inner circle . . 8
between the upper edg of the altar & the inner
ellipsis 9
between the inside of the grand entrance & the
jambs 9
between the two mortaises of the cornishes of the
cell 10
central distance in the uprights of the outer circle 6
height of the uprights of the outer circle . . . . $8\frac{1}{2}$
between each trilithon 5
length of the imposts of the outer circle 6
length of the cornishes of the cell 10
bredth of the trilithons 10
heigth of the uprights of the first trilithons . . . . [16, deleted]
        second . . . . [18, deleted]
        third . . . . [20, deleted]
aperture of the cell 23
length of the altar 10
length of the stone within the area at the entrance 12
the excentricity of the Cell 12
the bredth of the 2^d. trilithons 14
     3^d. 13
heigth of the stones of the inner circle 6

[103]

between jambs of the cell & center of the
grand entrance 20
between
the altar 30

the mean width of the inside of the cell 35
its length 40
between the middle of the altar & middle of the outer
circle behind the altar 40
the inner aperture of the outer wings of the cell 40
the outer length of the Cell 50
the lesser radius of the whole 50
the bredth of the avenue 40
the diameter of the temple 60
the radius that strikes the inside of the sides of the
cell 40
the bredth of the area 60
the diameter of the area 300
the diameter of the ditch environing the whole 360
the length of the avenue the strait part 2000
the length of the whole avenue . . . . [blank]
the length of the cursus 10000
from the inner edg of altar to outside of grand
entrance 60
from the outer jamb of cell to inside of outer circle . . . 10

They that please to compare these measures with the English scale or
the Roman & judg not what people to attribute this work too deserve
no conviction. The 360 that compleat the whole diameter have relation to the number of days in the year as then reckond.

Northeast long barrow near the river above Radfin [Ratfyn]
North long barrow
the long meta
west long barrow

[104]
ꝋ circle

Baculus cyclo coronatus ['bordered with upright rods'], signifyd among
the old Egyptians the process of the deity in right lines i.e. upon the
old elementary bodys. & tis no more than Homers golden chain &
that truly is only the principle of gravitation.

age piculu facito ut videatis omnes
['Come on, you gods, try me, if you like, and find out for
yourselves. Tie a golden rope to Olympus and take the other end of
it, all of you, gods and goddesses alike. Try as hard as you like, you
will never drag Zeus the high counsellor down from the skies to the
ground. But if I cared to pull in earnest from my end, I could haul
the lot of you up here, and the earth and sea as well. Then I would
make the rope fast to a spur of Olympus and leave everything to
dangle in mid-air']

Homer, Iliad, VIII, 19–26.

Figure 1

Thus tis represented in the Pamphylian obelus (Fig. 1) signifying the
descent of the triple deity the father, the word & the spirit to inferior
things. The wise Egyptians who were great geometricians by the line
& the circle could describe all things knowabl in nature, things that
were evidently to be seen & such as were only intellectually to be
understood. For tis plain invisibl things may be somwhat represented
by visibl but especially by the most simple & abstracted forms such as
mathematical figures conversant in numbers & geometry. & by thes
only the greatest genius's have rose to the highest pitch of knowledg
in sublime matters. Hence Boethius says let no one hope to attain the
knowledg of divine things that's a stranger to geometry. Pythagoras
Plato & the rest of the philosophic train plac'd the search after truth
in numbers & geometric figures & as thes things were part of the
study of the Druids tis no wonder we see vestiges of them in their
works. This is the beginning of [deleted] & the celestial power going
downwards before it begins to expand quaquaversum.

Y This part of the figure was an instrument very sacred among the
Egyptians being one of the props to the bier or are they carryd about
in their religious pomps to rest it upon when it stood, Pausanias in
Corinth mentions this *præibant aute sacrificuli sacris* struck *fusciuis*. ♂ signifys

the supreme being the only principle of all things, often occurs in
Egyptian monuments particularly on the *pamplylia obelisc* the *veran* or
barberine.[150]

[105]
Stadium

See the Lusitanians in Strabo.

From long meta.

at 1900 feet (579 m) the gate. 1900 more the entrance of west wing of
avenue

5350 (1631 m) thence to round meta.

1900 (579 m) at 1200 feet the strait part of avenue

1900	900 (274 m) more the gaps
———	1900 west wing of avenue
9150 (2789 m)	4000 (1219 m) to [round meta, deleted]

8000 (2438 m)   5350 from west end to

1702 (519 m) more to   entrance of west

——— round meta   wing of avenue

9702 feet (2957 m) which makes 5600 cubits the length
of 14 stadia, the length of the cursus. Each stadium 693 feet (211 m).
So that the cursus is 14 times the length of the greatest pyramid side.

8000 (2438 m)

1350 (412 m)

9350 (2850 m)

west wing of the avenue is 1800 feet (549 m).

[106]
Obelisc

Certainly it was not without reason that our wise & philosophic architects devised the different circles in our temple of different forms &
manner. The stones of the second & third rows are [obeliscs, deleted]
or rising from a square base to a point, tho' cut off before it comes
to it & this was derivd from the doctrin of the Egyptians so famd
[famed] for the stones of this nature of a stupendous bulk many
of which are now to be seen at Rome & other places. The latent
meaning of this figure in an obelisc is the nature of things or that
informd matter which has an innate appetite or capacity to receive
forms. & thus Abeneplius the Arabian says *Peripsam figuram pyramii*

['pyramidal shapes represent the primeval mother']. For as the obelisc is deducd from the upper point & so diffuses its self by lines into superficies & from thence into a solid dilating its self by degrees on all quarters: so the nature of all things from one principle & fountain indivisibl which is god the supreme workman by degrees takes various forms & comprehends all things connecting them to that one & first point. Whence they flowd. Which handsomly pictures the primogenial origin of the world deducd into that appearance we now behold. Thus matter created which has dimensions length bredth & thickness springs from a point indvisibl & thus the 4 elements or foundation of things is decypherd by this body of 4 sides. *Votaq pyramidu celsas solvuntur . . .* ['obelisks that reflect the constellations']. Lucan. The Chinese too have great veneration for obeliscs as Kircher shows *Jo.* I p.402.[151] It seems as if there were somewhat in the number 4 of obeliscs by that passage in Pliny *postea & alii regn in urbe.* So this *quatuor nº. quadrageno octo cubitoro,* ['the fourth of four, eight cubits high . . .'] the very light seems to have somewhat mystious, this relates to the 4 obeliscs at Burrowbridg. The obeliscs 40 seem to indicate the empyreal or sidereal world, the 20 the elementary. *Porta thausti flamuis.*[152]

The Kebla of the antients was mistaken for idolatry. Thus Maximus Tyrius says the Arabians worshipd he knew not what for he saw only a square stone.

[107]
Ambrosius

It has been a vulgar notion that Aurelius Ambrosius built this as a monument for the British nobility slain by the treachery of Hengist. Others that it was built by the Britains as a monument for Ambrosius himself slain by his enemys. Against this notion see Camdens annotator p.110. Against the town taking its name from Ambrosius, tis calld *pagus Imbri* by Matt. Westm. which has only a bare similitude in Domesday book tis calld Amblesbury. Geoffrey of Monmouth expressly calls it the monastery of Ambrius before any mention of Ambrosius. & that Ambrius the Abbot founded it. This he repeats again as a tradition but says it was upon the mountain of Ambrius VIII. 9. Now if there be any truth in this romantic history tis plain it was not namd from Ambrosius & the monastery being scituate in the meadows by the river side what he says of the mountain of Ambrius must be equally a fable. But all this notion is solidly confuted by Webb.

Witikind degest. *Saxonn I.* tells the story betwixt the Saxons & Thuringers & the watchword *nemet eour seaxes.*[153] From which probably our Amsbury story is borrowd, transferring that of the Saxons & Thuringians to the Saxons & our Britons.

Abrwsgl Amrosg signifys in Welsh *immensus ingeus* & I suppose to be the British name before the Saxons came in meaning the great temple, & thence came the storys of Aurelius Ambrosius & the like. Thus *main amber* a vast stone pitchd on an end in Cornwall I think, & hence the Ambrosiæ petræ at Tyre raisd by Hercules.

[108]

ovum

Great was the mystery of the oval form, & twas generally typical of the world, what secrets are comprehended in the oval thos know who are best acquainted with the secrets of the conic fectious of catoptrics, of the planetary motions. Eusebius *pampliulus III*[154] says an egg signifys the world, so its composition is analogous the yolk to the earth fecund with the seeds of things the white to the diaphanous air the shell to

Figure 2

the heavens that enclose all things. (Fig. 2) Thus tis upon the head of the lyonheaded figure in the bembin table a scarabeus included.[155] It signifys the solar power penetrating thro' the universe & fructifying it. The Egyptians made all their *sacræ tabulæ* oval, matters of great efficacy & prophylaetic, they were little boards like small tea tables whereon they carryd their cups & sacred vessels, & they were inscribd with sacred characters. V. *ouw* = *oroastren ap.* Plutarc. Besides an egg was a symbol of aereal substance & the seminary of aereal aials, here it has a regard to the sidereal or intellectual world. An egg was lypic of spmatical influx from the superior to inferior worlds.

Figure 3

The Egyptian sacred tables were generally of this form (Fig. 3) having a sort of foot at bottom, because usd sometimes to stand, sometimes without it of this form (Fig. 4)

Figure 4

Figure 5

nearer approaching to that of our cell, 5 times on the Ramessean obelisc or that now standing before the Church of St. John Lateran at Rome. (Fig. 5)

This oval figure of Stonehenge thus encompassd with circles shows the earth the nest of seminal principles encompassd or embrac'd by the celestial orbs thro' whose gates the divine influences of the archetypal mind descend thro' the sidereal worlds to the elementary. The sacra tabula of the Egyptians was propitiatory, as our adytum of the same form wherein the priests enterd as into others of the Hebrews &c to expiate for the sins of the people. Our figure is exactly of the shape of the sacræ tabulæ the foot of it is our opening. To this place belongs the words of Porphyry. *Egyptioru aute deori symbola taliasunt. Creatore Emepli (hemptha) dicunt, cuius imagine in forma bois faciunt colore cerules zona tenente & sceptru. Cuius in capile perma ponunt, significantes difficile inventu esse creatore & nemini conspicuu, vivificu elia & rege & intelligibli motu circulatu. Lic deus ab ore ovu pducit a quo nascitur deus que Egyptii Phta græci vulcanu appellant, significatur aute Egyptus ovo Mundus.*

Porphyry in *Enseb. III.7.* says the round figure is dedicate to eternity i.e. *Saturu chronus shadai*, as Abraham did.[156]

[109]
Gate
(Fig. 6)

The Druids in Stonehenge have a little more explicated their doctrine than elsewhere, which was much the same as that the Ægyptians. The imposts laid upon the others form a species of a door like the Thrones or tabernacles in the Bembin table which is emblematic of the world calld by Plutarch the house of Horus by the Ægyptians the great gate of the gods, for ever in temples

Figure 6

Figure 7

Figure 8

Figure 9

Figure 10

Figure 11

the frame of the world was to be regarded and in some measure imitated. Sometime the Egyptians expressd this by a man leaning over an altar as in the pamplilian obelisc, the characters of the sun (Fig. 7) & moon impressd, other times thus (Fig. 8) it signifys the influx of celestial upon terrestrial things.

The Egyptian hierogrammatists made great account of the gates of the world as they calld 'em, being the inlets of the divine influences of the superior powers upon the inferior world. Thes they expressd by a parallelogram figure sometime thus (Fig. 9) treble (Fig. 10) which they calld the great stations of the year sometime 9 in number, in their figure which they calld the mundane house very often 4 with an intermediate one thus (Fig. 11) & I suppose in our work the intermediate one is imitated by our obeliscs, for tis probabl Hermes Trismegistus made his first temples of stones & obeliscs like ours before arts in the settled Kingdom of Egypt rose to a considerable height & particularly that of architecture. So our druids followd still the most simple manner learnt first from their master.

II. *Kings XXIII.* 8. [Josiah 'defiled the high places where the priests had burned incense'].

[110]

The Druid measure or cubit was exactly the same as the Egyptian & Jewish: it was 1 foot & 4 fifths of our English measure or 20 inches & $\frac{4}{5}$. Hence measurd on the ground plot of Stonehenge. The semidiameters that form'd the respective circles in the chalk were of 30 cubits the length of the altar stone & the bredth of each trilithon is 10 cubits. The grand entrance is $2\frac{1}{2}$. The ordinary intervals of the outer circle are 2. The bredth of the outer stones 4. Between the outer circle & pyramidal circle 5. The grand entrance of the pyramidal circle $2\frac{1}{2}$ the aperture of the cove 25. The bredth of 2 stones of the outer circle with the interval 10. The bearings from long meta by the compass

Radfin [Ratfyn] 109.

Prophets 225.

Bush Barrow 226

Stonehenge 230½

North long barrow 334.

[111]
Radfin [Ratfyn]

qua se subducere colles . . . ['leads down the slope to the water']

Fin in the Old Irish is white. The white road, vadu.

Patriarchal

Pausanias says the Thracians usd to build temples to Sol of a round form open at top. These in reality were patriarchal dedicated to EL or god almighty But in time the devil & the contagion of their neighbors made them idolators. Pliny XXII speaks of British women daubing over their bodys with glastu & going naked in some religious solemnitys.[157]

> *Similis plantagini glastum in Gallia*
>
> ['There is a plant called glastum with which [British women] stain all their body, and at certain religious ceremonies march along naked, with a colour resembling that of Ethiopians']
>
> Pliny, *Natural History, XXII, ii.*

He means either the Britanni of the continent, for he speaks of an herb growing in Gaul: or else he means the Gallic colonys in Brittan. Dionys. Perieg.[158] mentions the same of the British. women on the continent celebrating the orgia of Bacchus crying *evole* ['fly']. They had learnt it of later Phænician traders who had it of the Canaanitish nations in imitation of somewhat they had observd in the Jews. A remarkable instance in our Druids of patriarchal institution, either they learnt it of Jacob or they both learnt it from same comon original, as of Abraham not unlikely, of crossing their hands in a religious way when they gatherd the misletoe as Pliny informs us. Their crucifying a man at one of their Great festivals & in the temple, is a wonderful tho' horrid notion of the sacrifice of the Messiah.

[113]
Obliquity

The entrance of Stonehenge is 4 degrees East from the true Northeast point.[159] They set it to the Northeast because that is the suns utmost elongation in somer sostices when they held a grand festival & made games like the Isthunian. It varyd because of the compass. 6 degrees East from Northeast. I take the obliquity to be barely 4 degrees long meta varys 4 degrees from North & south.

Points to 3 degrees Old Kings Barrows & Aurelius.

From Bush Barrow
Stonehenge 32
North long barrow 19.
Little barrow west I opend $353\frac{1}{2}$
middle of New 7 Kings $58\frac{1}{2}$.
Haradon 80.
1 King $81\frac{1}{2}$.
Prophets 215
West long barrow 275.
More southern group 170.
Barrow Lord Pembroke opend 91.

[113]
bearings from Stonehenge

Salisbury steeple directly south
North long barrow 10 degrees eastward of the north point 365.
Meridian line.
Long meta 55.60 5 degrees variation 20 degrees east of northeast.
r. meta $300.\frac{1}{2}$ 20 degrees west of northwest.
1st. barrow I opened 334. Queen Barrow.
Midlemost of 7 Kings Barrows fulle.
3 little barrows north of cursus its center the north point.
Rabit barrows west south west.
Bush Barrow 211.
Rabbit barrow 251.

one King Barrow 118.

Salisbury steeple 168

midlemost of new 7 Kings barrows 90. East Haradon barrow in the same line.

[114]
Area

The northwest stone of vallum is 25 feet (7.6 m) from edg of the ditch. 85 (26 m) to the [incomplete] at round meta Stoneheng is 117 (35.7 m).

7 New Kings Barrows stand in the meridian line.

[115]
Cursus

About the tumulus of Drusus on the banks of the Rhine they run courses upon a certain day of the year annually & the citys of Gaul publickly solemnizd the sacred *sueton*. Claudius.I. An altar was built there, which the Germans afterward destroyd. Germanicus restor'd it, & to the honor of his father ran races himself with the legions. Tacitus *Ann. 2.7.3.*[160]

> ['He restored the altar and himself headed the legions in the celebrations in honour of his father']
>
> Tacitus, *Annals, V, vii.*

[119]
Irish

The storys of Stonehenge being brought from Ireland is of the same kind with all Welsh storys, when they would express anything exceedingly old & beyond any memory, they say immediately the Irish did it, it was in the line of the Irish &c. Which plainly means no more than that the old Britons after the Roman times understood it to be done by the most ancient inhabitants who went into Ireland. Or of the same race that peopled Ireland. This was afterwards like all other things of strange nature turnd into Merlins Magic. & trackd to the monkish legends of Ambrosius because of the adjacent town of Amsbury which they pretend had its name from him. It may probably enough be affirmd that Ambrosius livd at Sorbuodunum

[Roman Salisbury] & not at this place where was no security in those perillous times. I doubt not but this town is no more than the bury or more properly berry upon the Avon that is the farm. Thus Upper Avon [Upavon] and Nether Avon [Netheravon] higher up the river.

After this manner is Merlin introducd speaking to the king, by such writers as Winkin de Woord *fract. temp.*[161] soth seyde Merlyn but in all your lande ben none suche. For giauntes sette them for grete good of themself. For atte every tyme that they were wounde or in any manner hurle they wysshe the stones with hole water & thenne they wysshe them therwyth & anone they were hoole. Now tis not improbable that if there be any truth of the story of Hengists meeting the British princes hereabouts (tho' I rather look upon it to be too farr off Hengists country & interest in Kent) that they might meet near Stonehenge tho not at the place because that would be lyable to treachery but when the assignation was in the middle of these wide downs no place so proper so notorious as Stonehenge.

Mr Marten[162] gives us abundance of instances of vulgar supestition now retaind of stones laid on an altar in the church which should obtain a medicinal virtue thence, this is Druidish relique. So the water of wells in our religious houses may be reckond among these ceremonious cures for a saints name annexd adds much virtue. The dust of S⟨t⟩. Michaels Mount near Hereford sluice of much efficacy. The same holy craft has run thro' all nations & ages. Whether to enrich themselves or to bring people to a house of religion. Alexand. Necham says *Fluic tanta munus suscepit Hibernia gaudens* ['In Ireland service is freely given to the strength of stones'].

Wells city a remnant of Belgæ as well as Devizes of Divitiacus.

[118]

I shall conclude thus, that the greatness & the beauty of these Works are the most incontestable proofs of Cæsars assertion about our Druids Disciplina in Britannia reperta &c. In vain doe German or French writers endeavor to spirit away the sense of that great Author because they would have nothing said to the honor of Britain. Cæsar is clear in the point the discipline that is the doctrine the collegiate way of life the æconomy the study was all of British invention. No doubt but the order of Druids came from the East of the continent.

But the priests in comparison to ours were like their works rude &
unpolishd. Cæsar dos not speak his opinion only which he might
perhaps imagine himself, but he adds matter of fact so notorious as
cannot be eluded, the Gauls sent their youth yearly into Britain to be
instructed there. It was not possible for him to be mistaken here or to
invent it. That the Gauls were ignorant of the British polity & country
of their methods of war ports &c as Cæsar say IIII. is no argument
against himself but by either of these answers is sufficiently disannuld
[disproven] 1. The Gauls would not discover their knowledg of the
particularitys Cæsar enquird after, they pretended ignorance, because
twas not their interest to have them conquerd, for they sent succors to
the Gauls as Cæsar mentions more than once & it was their last refuge
& retiring place if they could not fit easy under a Roman yoak & twas
as easy for them to say they knew nothing of the matter as otherwise
& twas as honest. 2.¹⁶³ Tis not to be supposd that tho' the youth of
Gaul were sent into Britain for education that therefore they should
return fully apprizd of the government manners ports warlike customs
& the like of the Island Cæsar acquaints us with what is sufficient to
contradict this notion, for suppose such young men as these were
capable of learning all these affairs & making proper enquirys, the
strictness of life, the long confinement the secrecy & methods of institution the Druids had makt it absolutely impossible they should know
any thing beyond the wood the hamlet where thes discoverys were
they could not ramble about from town to town from one court to
another or if they had would have able to give no better an account at
their return than most of our young gentlemen when the[y] have been
the fashionable tour of France & Italy. If we see

[120]

these stupendous works in Britain where so much art & order
elegance & contriveance is displayd & none like them upon the continent, no more to be compard with ours than ours to the Ephesian
temple certainly the reason lyes upon the same climax we were as
superior to them in art as the Greeks to us, & credite operibus is proof
sufficient & full conviction, if I may be allowd after the thought I
have employd about this matter & the pains will entitle me to be a
competent judg.

Brytan signifys the country of the Brygians or Phrygians so that the customs in Homer *quadrate* [equate] much with those of the antient Brytans.

[121]

cursus − 74. 105[164]
area − 114.
tumuli − 95.
cavitys 78. 94.
funeral games 98.
avenues. 97.
enginry − 99.
gate − 109.
Ambrosius. 107.
Radfin [Ratfyn] − 111. Patriarchal 60.

urn burial. 86. 96.
beads. 92.
burning bodys 100.
♂. 104.
obelisc 106.
Egg − 108.
measure 110.
obliquity − 113.
bearings from Stonehenge 113.

[122]

The Reader will percieve that the many drawings I made of these veiws upon the plain are for pure necessity to give the reader an exact notion of the whole thing, tho' they must needs make but a poor appearance, there being no variety of objects to please the eye in sketches of those extended plains. Besides it was necessary this way to perpetuate the vestiges of this celebrated wonder & of the barrows avenues cursus &c for I foresee that it will in a few years be universally plowed over & consequently defacd. Large allowances must be made for the Author if this work appears a little inconnected, for so great as its extent so wholly untouchd before & so great variety of thoughts perpetually crouded upon the mind in so copious a scene of New Antiquitys: that it should rather be the work of an age than the product of part of the amusement of so few years since I began to think of these things, & I durst look upon it myself only as a ground-work of future disquisition a withdrawing of the curtain of Antient times to open a full view of the greatness of thought in our Predecessors whoever they were, that the nearer we look into them the more they surprize & puzzle us.

Abury is a bold & masterly drawing like that of a hand secure of sufficient exactness, Stonehenge like that of a nice & correct copyist.

In nothing more did I ever observe the greatness & simple Majesty that is peculiar to the works of the Ancients than in these Celtic monuments.

The excellency of works consists much in imitation of those of creation which are of eternal date & need no reparation & herein the Celts have been remarkably great in design in execution & duration for what else is Abury, & stones seems as if it had been created on the spot to more than vulgar people.

Mr Jay of Nettlecomb [Nettlecombe] wrote somewhat about Stone-henge of which Mr Paschal speaks.[165]

The little wooden *ædes* [temples] of the Eleans mentiond by Pausanias & quoted by Webb by all says our Author is agreed to be a sepulchre.

[123]

When we behold & consider thes vast works about the Kingdom which I call Celtic, whereof we have no shadow of history, we must enquire what great people livd here in antient times who possibly could be authors of them, & we shall not be far to seek after we are acquainted the Druids were here most famous for antiquity & discipline, & that by the greatest authority imaginabl even he that first made an inroad upon the Island & opend to the learned world the secret recesses of thos famous priests & philosophers who from times immemorial had here livd fresh from servile labour & undisturbed in their great studys: such as he mentions in his commentarys. it will be questioned when thes people in all appearance had not so much art as to build houses but dwelt in woods & rocks or at best in mud wall cottages, how they should be thought to rear thes structures, but to that tis easy to answer that the very works themselves demonstrates they were the effect of such people, because they are not of stones dug out of a quarry & chizeld to scantlings, or disposd after the manner of Edifices with roofs & rooms & the like. They are of materials laid ready to their hands in the open air upon the surface of the earth, & where thes are obvious, there we find thes works.[166] They had nothing further to doe but to make their design & pick out such stones as were nearly of a size fit for their intention, & then by strength to raise & transport them to their proper places. This indeed requird some art & some degree of machinery & that was part of their studys. Thes men who livd in colleges & communitys seperate from the vulgar, may be supposd to spend their time not altogether in idleness nor many ages & successions but in considering the powers of nature & communicating the result of their enquirys one to another & so thro' long tracts of time of laying the foundation of the sciences of Geometry & mechanics & mathematics as we find in Greece & other nations, who from infancy at length brought them to good perfection. Further it highly behovd thes abstracted students by such works to keep up the great opinion the vulgar had of their learning & sanctity & authority. For if they saw nothing producd by them & nothing extraordinary they would soon grow into contempt the more won-derful therefore were their productions the more veneration would be securd to their order & an *implicite* [implicit] execution of their com-mands. Upon thes motives doubtless they set about thes prodigious works. As they were the ministers of the gods it was natural & con-venient to display somewhat of their capacity in providing some remarkabl places for their public meetings to doe sacrifices & other rites, & whether all the countrys round should resort at certain seasons as a national act or that of a certain region or principality.

[124]

Now to perform such works tis plain that some art & much strength is all thats necessary. Men they had innumerabl & that would not be slack in lending their utmost power in the case when they were told the great blessings from above that attended such services. It was not difficult for men of a good genius to invent methods to regulate & assist the strength so as to bring their work to good conclusion.[167] The power of the leaver is the first the most notorious in nature & what they could not be ignorant & that is sufficient for the purpose. We may readily imagin that half a score leavers made of long timbers trees applyd all around one of thes stones would raise it so as that they might place rollers underneath it & so either by repeated protrusion or by pulling it with many ropes & hands transport it whether they pleasd besides in many operations of this sort experience would necessarily im prove them & make the work more easy. & in particular I would propose this way of doing it among others which is as simple as any & as effectual. First let their be prepard a frame of timber whereon the stone is to rest & to which it is to be fastned after this manner, of the full bulk of the stone suppose 20 feet (6.1 m) long 16. feet (4.9 m) broad, upon which the stone is laid, thes timbers may be a foot (Fig. 12) & half in diameter fastned into one another with pins, this is to be laid on rollers, which are to slide upon another timber work upon the ground & made rough at bottom with snags, so that it won't slip. The two outsides of this frame must be

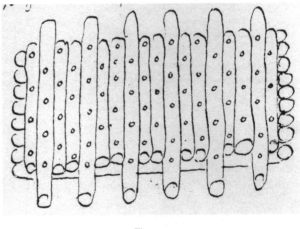

Figure 12

formd like the bench of oars in a galley & plyd with leavers in the nature of a galley oars, two or 3 of thes lower works being ready to set one before another, the stone would thus as effectually be carryd by land as the ship by water, with great ease & delight especially when the men by practise came to be expert at the business & I doubt not but Fontana's obelisc[168] might thus have been workd without his pompous apparatus.

[125]

(Fig. 13)

This frame laid upon the ground as we said & fixt to it either by the snags & its own weight or by stakes drove in at the end will be the opposition to the protruded stone by the perpetual action of the

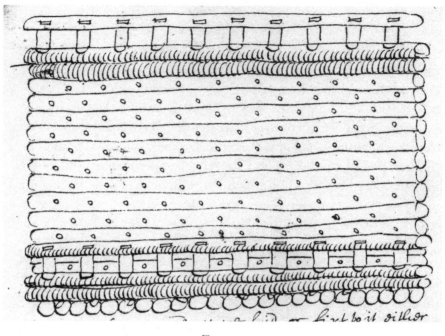

Figure 13

leavers moving all at once till the stone is pushd on to another such framd & prepard with leavers in like manner. I would advise that all the leavers of a side be coupled together by a light pole running across them & fastned to every one with that the motion & force be preservd uniform & entire.

If it be thought that this timber would prove as heavy & difficult to carry as the stone its self, I can say nothing to that till tryal be made how great strength of timber is necessary for the work but in such case another method I would propose to draw the stones on a frame of timber with rollers fitted to it in nature of wheels. this must be brought under the stone when elevated by the force of leavers a height sufficient from the ground then by ropes & a quantity of men it may be drawn to any distance. & all this is extremely favord by the fine downy country here. For the setting up these stones into their proper seats I judg, the best way would be to enclose them first in a square yoke of timber & raise them by several leavers so that whilst suspended in the air the little stones may be (Fig. 14)

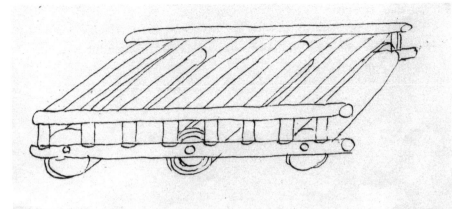

Figure 14

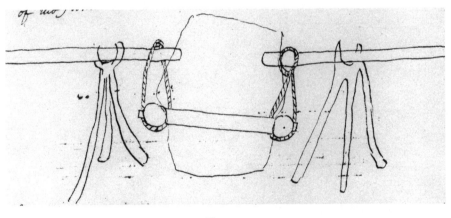

Figure 15

[126]

rightly set at bottom for a sure basis & thus they may be drawn up &
let down at pleasure for frequent tryals till settled to satisfaction & this
notion is much favourd by the very shape of the stones (Fig. 15)
beside. Leavers may be multiplyd if occasion requires as other
mechanic powers so as to overcome any weight given according to
Archimedes' assertion.

Sunt mihi, pars montis, vivo pendentia saxo
['I have a whole mountainside for my possessions, deep caves in the
living rock, where neither the sun is felt in his midsummer heat,
nor the winter's cold']

Ovid, *Metamorphoses* XIII, dcccx–xii.

APPENDIX 1

Unnumbered loose sheets inserted into the manuscript relating to Stonehenge.

[sheet 1]

Mr Herbert in Broadway Westm^r. chapel street has an original presentation book of Inigo Jones's *Stonehenge* to my Lord Thumond the presentation in MS.

$$\begin{array}{r} 1656 \\ 210 \\ \hline 1866 \end{array}$$

[sheet 2]

7 New Kings Barrows

Figure 16

Ikening Street derives its name not from beginning but ending at the Iceni, -via Iceniana or the way from the south to the Iceni. That turn in Cranburn [Cranborne] Chase is a plain demonstration the road began from the south. From this to Vindegladia tis as strait as an arrow & very beautiful. 2 old flat barrows by the termination of Stonehenge avenue. The 2^d. intake of the Belgae was to secure their conquests upon the Rivers about Wilton. & then that was made the capital.

The New Kings Barrows generally 530 at bottom in circuit. i.e. 100 cubits in diameter. 400 cubits was a stadium antiently according to villalpand. 14 of these the length of cursus 9800 feet (2987 m). Abury each avenue is 10 stadia 7000 foot (2134 m).

100	100	400
35	50	400
—	—	400
500	000	400
300	500	400
		1400
3500	8) 5000 (10	400
		2800

[sheet 3]

[Sheet 3 is an incomplete index to the manuscript. None of the illustrations, or 'tableaux', is contained in the manuscript, but the descriptions no doubt refer to sketches and plans which were later engraved and printed in *Stonehenge, A Temple Restor'd to the British Druids*, published in 1740.]

[reverse of sheet 3]
index

APPENDIX 2

Unnumbered loose sheets inserted into the manuscript that do not relate to Stonehenge.

(i) A newspaper cutting dated April 1754 relating the discovery of a human skeleton during the levelling of a barrow by labourers on 15 April on Durnford Downs, near Salisbury.

(ii) A drawing and description of Sir Richard Bewforest's tomb and a report on the promontory fort Dike Hills and Sinodun Camp hillfort at Little Wittenham, Oxfordshire, dated September 1736.

(iii) A double-sided sheet of compass bearings taken from positions in and around Avebury, Wiltshire.

(iv) A sheet containing 'The Canon for finding the Suns Amplitude'.

(v) A double-sided sheet concerning 'Druidical Remains in the Isle of Jersey', apparently copied from an unknown source.

(vi) A sheet concerning classical references to chariots.

(vii) A double-sided sheet, the first side regarding Roman coins, the reverse an incomplete plan of an unnamed town or city.

NOTES

INTRODUCTION. THE HISTORY OF THE MANUSCRIPT

(Where a work is cited in the Bibliography only the author, date (if necessary) and pages are cited here. e.g. Note 7, Piggott, 1985, 46, 50–1, 87–9, is an abbreviation for: S. Piggott, (1985) *William Stukeley. An Eighteenth-Century Antiquary*, 2nd edition, Thames & Hudson, London).

1   Provenance of Stukeley's manuscripts: Haycock, 263–4.
2   Britton: *Memoir of John Aubrey, F. R. S.*, Wilts Top Soc, 1845, Preface, vi.
3   Stukeley's descendant: G. Clement Whittick, *Antiquity 7*, 1933, 222–6.
4   Lukis: *I–III*, 1882–7.
5   R. F. St Andrew St John of Ealing: *Compact Edition of the National Dictionary of Biography, II*, Oxford University Press, 1975, 2027.
6   Ms. 4. 253: information from J. Brynmor Jones, Local Studies Librarian, Cardiff, 31 May 2002; and Daniel Huws, former Keeper of Manuscripts, Cardiff, 4 December 2002.
7   'The History . . . ': Piggott, 1985, 46, 50–1; 87–9; Haycock, 128–9. See also his: 'The questionable reputation of Dr William Stukeley', *3rd Stone 45*, 2003, 16–21.
8   Piggott's archaeological caution: Haycock 7. But R. Hayman, *Riddles in Stone: Myths, Archaeology and the Ancient Britons*, Hambledon, 1997, 142.
9   Haycock on archaeology and history: 9, 183. M. Hunter, *John Aubrey and the Realm of Learning*, Duckworth, 1975, 159–60.
10   Sir Thomas More's *History* . . . as history: C. Ross, *Richard III*, Methuen, 1990, xxvi–vii. see also: K. Dockray, *Richard III. A Source Book*, Sutton, 1997, xxiii; P. Kendall, *Richard the Third*, Allen & Unwin, 1955, 399; Horace Walpole, *Historic Doubts on the Life and Reign of Richard the Third*, ed. P. W. Hammond, Sutton, 1987, 26.
11   Ucko et al, 74–92.
12   Caesar and the Druids: *Gallic Wars*, Book VI, 13.
13   John Aubrey and the Druids: *Aubrey I*, 129. also 133, 135.

WILLIAM STUKELEY (1687–1765)

1   Stukeley, 1776a, 51–61, 'Itinerarium Cimbricum'.
2   Copper kettle: C. S. Briggs, *Antiquaries Journal 57*, 1977, 91.
3   Piggott, 1985, 45; 1989, 125.
4   Burl, 'John Aubrey's 'Monumenta Britannica', a review article, *Wiltshire Archaeological & Natural History Magazine*, 77,

1982, 163–6.

5   Lukis, *III*, 1887, 273.

6   The lie: Burl, *Prehistoric Avebury*, 2002, 47; Piggott, 1985, Note 3, 45–6.

7   Giants: J. Michell, *Megalithomania*, Thames & Hudson, London, 1982, 44–5. Henry of Huntingdon, *Historia Anglorum*, 1130, trans. T. Forester, Llanerch Press, Felinfach, 1991, 7. Geoffrey of Monmouth, *Historium Regum Britanniae*, c. 1147, trans L. Thorpe, Folio Society, London, 1969, 172–5.

8   'Antiquities', Aubrey, 1980, 25; 'a Conjurer': Aubrey: *Wiltshire. The Topographical Collections, 1659–70*, edited, J. E. Jackson, Wiltshire Archaeological & Natural History Society, Devizes, 1862, 4; Camden, *Britain . . .* , G. Latham, London, 1637, 9.

9   G. Daniel, *The Idea of Prehistory*, Pelican, Harmondsworth, 1964, 19.

10 William Shakespeare: 'As You Like It', c. 1599–1600, IV, I, 97–8.

11 Caesar, *The Gallic War*, V, 14, 253; VI, 13, 337, trans. H. J. Edwards, Heinemann, London, 1979. Tacitus, *On Britain and Germany*, XI, 61, trans. H. Mattingly, Penguin, Harmondsworth, 1948. Other classical authors on Britain: *H. Sharpe, Britain B.C. As Described in Classical Writings*, Williams & Norgate, London, 1910.

12 'Temples of the druids': Aubrey, 1980, 25. 'less salvage': Aubrey, *Wiltshire Topographical Collections*, Note 8, 5.

13 Letter to Archbishop Wake: Wiltshire Record Office, Colt Hoare Collection, 38 3/907.

14 Falsified measurements: Piggott, 1985, 106–7; Stanton Drew avenues: J. Rickman, 'On the antiquity of Avebury and Stonehenge', *Archaeologia 28*, 1840, 401.

15 Haycock, 2002, 7; M. Hunter, *Science and Society in Restoration England*, Cambridge University Press, 1981, 190; Ucko et al., 54. A contrary belief in Stukeley's pre-Christian druids appears in Sweet, 2004, 128–131. Toland, she argued, believed that druids were the prototypes for the Christian priesthood but not Christians themselves, and 'Stukeley always entertained a favourable opinion of Toland's druidical writings, if not his religious beliefs'.

16 Stukeley to Wake, 3 June 1729: Lukis, *I*, 1882, 216.

17 Bodleian Library: MS Eng. Misc. c. 323, f. 140.

18 Snakes in Egypt: M. Lurker, *The Gods and Symbols of Ancient Europe*, Thames & Hudson, 1980: Amun, 25–6, 108. Cleopatra: Burl, *Catullus. A Poet in the Rome of Julius Caesar*, Constable & Robinson, London, 2004, 219; Stukeley and Egyptian gods: see Notes, n. 156.

19 The Sanctuary 'ovals': Piggott, 1935, 22–32. The falsified plan of the Sanctuary concentric 'ovals': Stukeley, 1743, Tab. XX, 38.

20 Whiston, (1667–1752): Piggott, 1989, 39; Haycock, 197–206.

21 Toland, (1670–1722). He evaluated the accepted and apocryphal religions. To many of his contemporaries this was blasphemy. *A Critical History . . .* , 2nd edition, 1814, 135, Lackington, Hughes & Harding, London.

22 Toland and Stukeley: Piggott, 1950, 16–17, 119–20; 1989, 141.

23 The 'proto-Christian Druids': Stukeley, 1740, 53, 63. Also: Stukeley, 1743, 90.

24 Letter of 1729 to Roger Gale: Lukis, *I*, 228.

25 Removal of the Stonehenge avenue: Stukeley, 1722–4, MS Eng. Misc. c. 323, f.129. Roger Gale's letter about the omission of avenue stones, 1740: Lukis, *III*, 268.

26 James I and Stonehenge: Jones, 1655, 1–2.

27 The smashed portal stones: Jones, 1655, 57.

28 The Aubrey Hole cavities: Aubrey, 1980, 80, Plate VII. The 'avenue': ibid.

29 The Slaughter Stone: Stone, 1924, 122.

30 The graded heights of avenue stones: Burl, 2000, 327 et al. No stones missing since 1747: Petrie, 1880, 16.

31 The avenue: Jones, 1655, 55, 57, Plate n. 2; Aubrey, 1980, 59, Plate VIII, 81. Evidence for the avenue: Castleden, 1993, 131–2. Geo-physical surveys of the avenue: Bartlett & David, *Proc Prehistoric Soc 48*, 1982, 90–3; David & Payne, in *Science & Stonehenge*, eds. Cunliffe, B. & Renfrew, C., Oxford University Press, London, 1997, 76–7, 82–3.

32 Its date: Cleal et al., 1985 ± 50 BC; 1728 ± 68 BC; 1915 ± 40 BC; 1770 ± 70 BC, in a radio-carbon chronology and about 2400 ± 75 BC in calendar years. For a provisional chronology for avenues in Britain and Ireland, (2600–2000 BC) see: Burl, *From Carnac to Callanish. The Prehistoric Stone rows and Avenues of Britain, Ireland and Brittany*, Yale University Press, 1993, 23.

33 Proof of the Beckhampton, Avebury avenue: *Wiltshire Archaeological & Natural History Magazine, 93*, 2000, 1–8.

34 Stukeley's plans of the avenue: Bodleian Library, Gough Maps 229: August, 1721, f. 16; June 6, 1724, f. 24. The Heel Stone and bowing: Stukeley, 1740, 33–4.

35 Druid Cubit: Stukeley, 1740, 6, 15. Megalithic Yard, A. Thom, 'The megalithic unit of length', *Megalithic Sites in Britain*, Oxford University Press, 1967, 34–55.

36 'Through a glass, darkly', *Corinthians XIII: 12*, Bodleian MS Eng. Misc. c.323, 139.

37 Site of Stukeley's burial: F. W. Steer, *Antiquity XXV*, 1951, 213–14.

38 Arthur Mee, *The King's England. Essex*, Hodder & Stoughton, London, 1940. The burial places of Aubrey and Stukeley: M. Kerrigan, *Who Lies Where? A Guide to Famous Graves*, Fourth Estate, London, 1995: Aubrey, p.125; Stukeley, p. 288.

39 Stukeley's coffin: *in litt.* January 2003, D. W. Large, Church Archivist, East Ham.

STONEHENGE

References in these Notes that are not cited in the Bibliography are listed at the end of this section. In the text they are indicated by an asterisk*.

1 Michael Drayton. *Poly-Olbion, III*, xxii, 1613, 40–1:
On Salisbury Plain
. . . , that Stonehenge there should stand.

She, first of plains; and that,
first wonder of the land. (Long,
1876, 187)*.

2 Caesar, *The Gallic War*, Book II,
4*: Diviciacus of the Suessiones
tribe held land near modern
Soissons in northern France.
(Commius, Book IV, 21).

3 Dr Edmund Halley (1656–1742),
astronomer and mathematician.
Friend of Stukeley. In 1687 he
published a catalogue of stars in
the southern hemisphere. He
later predicted the return of the
comet named after him, and
encouraged Sir Isaac Newton to
publish his *Principia*.

4 'Bristol stones'. Geologically
Stukeley referred to a mixture of
dolerites and other stones from
the Preseli range in south-west
Wales. The 'great stones' were
sarsens from north Wiltshire.
The Altar Stone was a mica-
ceous sandstone from
Wales.

5 'Glewy sort'. As late as the early
seventeenth century there was a
widespread belief that stones as
large as the sarsens of Stonehenge were artificial. In
Camden's *Britain*, 1637, 253, 'Yet
some there are, that thinke
theme to bee no naturall stones
hewne out of the rocke, but arti-
ficially made of pure sand, and
by some glewie and unctuous
matter knit and incorporate
together', like others Camden
had seen in Yorkshire.

6 Philip Sidney, 'The Countess of
Pembroke's Arcadia', written at
Wilton, 1580, for his sister Mary,
'being done in loose sheets of
paper, most of it in your presence, the rest by sheets sent you
as fast as they were done'.

(Lever, *The Herberts of Wilton*,
42, 48–9)*.
Neer Wilton sweet huge
heapes of stones are found
But so confus'd that neither
any eye
Can count them just, nor
reason reason try
What force them brought
to so unlikely ground.
(Chippindale, 1994, 45).

7 Henry of Huntingdon, *Historia
Anglorum*, c. 1130: 'The second
[wonder] is at Stonehenge,
where stones of extraordinary
dimensions are raised as
columns . . .'. (Forester, 1991, 7)*.

8 Stonehenge Danish: In his book
Chorea Gigantum of 1663, Walter
Charleton (1619–1707), physician
to Charles II and a colleague
of John Aubrey, argued that
Stonehenge had been built by
the Danes.

9 A nunnery: at Amesbury near
Stonehenge. Arthur's wife,
Guinevere, was rumoured to
have retired there after the
king's death (Ashe, 1980,
5–6)*.

10 Vespasian's Castle, Amesbury:
an Iron Age hillfort centred on
SU 145 417.

11 Normanton and pewter at
Wilsford-cum-Lake: (Aubrey,
1982, 708–9).

12 '7 barrows together': The New
King bowl barrows centred on
SU 134 421.

13 'Elegant bell-like shape'. Stukeley referred to the Wessex
'fancy' barrows: *Bells*, large
banked and ditched round
barrows; *Discs*, the 'little rising',
delicately small, round barrows
with female burials at the centre

of a wide, banked circular plateau. (Grinsell, 1978, 27–30).

14 Twin bell-barrows: Wilsford South, SU 117 398. (Grinsell, 1978, 36).

15 Sir Andrew Fountaine, (1676–1753) an antiquarian who succeeded Isaac Newton as warden of the Mint in 1727.

16 Inigo Jones (1573–1652) architect, whose book *Stone-Heng*, 1655, argued that Stonehenge was built by the Romans. John Aubrey (1626–1697), author of *Brief Lives* and the first person to undertake serious fieldwork at Stonehenge and Avebury noted many architectural errors in Jones's arguments.

17 'Weathers' are sarsen stones. From a distance they can resemble grazing sheep or 'grey wethers'.

18 The chronological calculations. Around 1740 Stukeley believed the magnetic variation at Stonehenge was about 11°, an error of some −3°. Unluckily he had used a faulty theodolite. (Atkinson, 1985), Unaware of it he attempted to date Stonehenge by calculations based on the variation from east to west back to east, a cycle that Halley told him lasted seven hundred years.

In his chronology Stukeley was constrained by the early eighteenth century belief that the world was hardly 6,000 years old, an estimate based on Bishop Ussher's mid-seventeenth century calculation of 4004 BC. Thinking that three of Halley's 700-year cycles, 2100 years, would bring him close to the date of Stonehenge he picked a reliable historical benchmark from which to calculate. He chose an important date, 753 BC, AUC or *Ab Urbe Condita*, the year in which Rome was founded. By a minor error, Stukeley used 752 BC. AUC is also offered as 'The year of the foundation of the city, *Anno Urbis Conditae*'. Inconsistently, he also used AUC as 'the foundation of', 'before the foundation' and 'after the foundation'.

On page 13 of the manuscript the results of his computations were: **AD 1692**: 1692–1400 (2 × 700) = 292 AD + 752 = AUC 1044. 1044 − 700 = 344 BC. AUC 753 − 344 = 409 BC, a possible date for the building of Stonehenge. **AD 1634**: 1634 − 1400 = 234 AD + 753 = AUC 987, 234 years before 753 BC. 987 − 700 = 287. AUC 752 − 287 = 465 BC, a second possible date for Stonehenge.

AD 1620: 1620 − 1400 = 220 AD + 752 = 972, 220 years before the AUC of Rome in 752 BC. 972 was also APJ, *Ante Partus Jesus*, 972 years before Christ was born. 972 − 700 = 272 after AUC, 479 'years before our Saviour's birth', an arithmetical approximation to his own 972 − 700 = 272 or 481 years after Rome, a third 'date' for Stonehenge.

To add to the mathematical chaos, Stukeley carelessly wrote 418 instead of 481 to ensure the head-aching confusion of later researchers. Of the three possibilities, 409, 465, and 481 BC, Stukeley preferred the last. He believed that the Belgic king, 'Divitiacus', had thrown up the Wansdyke earthwork in 100 BC some 650 years after the foundation of Rome and then expelled the Stonehenge druids from Salisbury Plain, excluding them from Stonehenge. The sarsen circle, therefore, had been used from about 480 to 100 BC, 380 years, quite long enough to account for the many barrows around the ring.

Everything was wrong. Wansdyke, 'Wodin's ditch', consisted of fifty WSW–ENE miles of defensive bank and ditch stretching roughly from Bristol to Marlborough. It was probably a late sixth-century AD earthwork against invading Saxons. It had an improbable association with Aurelius Ambrosius, a late fifth-century AD pre-Arthurian British war-leader.

Stukeley was in error by at least five centuries. Wansdyke had nothing to do with the historical Diviciacus who 'within living memory' of 57 BC had been king of all Gaul and part of Britain. Ironically, had Stukeley followed Halley's belief (page 23 here) that the ring had stood for at least three thousand years, and chosen six rather than three cycles of seven hundred years used six the figure of 4200 – 1740 would have given 2640 BC, a date close to the range of calibrated radio-carbon dates for the sarsen ring, 2562–2191 BC. (Cleal et al, 524–5).

19 Stukeley's Celtic Cubit of 20.8″ derived from the Egyptian 20.6″ and Hebrew measure of 20.8″. The Roman Foot was 11.65″, (52.8, 52.1, 52.8, 29.6 cm).
Page 17 shows Stukeley at his arithmetical worst. He must be credited with being the first to

deduce that the builders of prehistoric stone circles had used a unit of measurement, his Celtic Cubit, thereby anticipating Alexander Thom's Megalithic Yard by over two centuries. Sadly, unlike his meticulous successor, he was cavalier in his application of his units, which he proposed as a cubit of 20.8″, a palm one-sixth of a cubit, $3\frac{1}{2}$″, and a staff of six cubits, 10′5″ (3.2 m). He also accepted English feet and inches. (Stukeley, 1740, 6–7, 11–12, Tab. VI, 'the scale of cubits and feet compar'd', and 15–16).

The results were rarely accurate. On page 17 the lintel over the north-east entrance, stone 130, was 11′11″ long (3.63 m) which Stukeley said was 7 cubits 4 palms or 13′4″ (4.1 m), a discrepancy of 1′5″. Other miscalculations on the page included 136′ (41.5 m) being 80 cubits or 138′6″ (42.2 m); and 120′9″ (36.8 m) being 70 cubits or 121′4″ (37 m).

In his book of 1740, 11–12, Stukeley shrugged off the contradictions: 'Tis not to be suppos'd, that in the work, the minuteness of *Desgodetz*, with which he measur'd the remains of old *Rome* is expected or even possible' because at Stonehenge the intractable sarsens had never been precisely shaped, had been exposed to centuries of weather and then damaged by vandals. The explanation permitted Stukeley the latitude to argue for former original prehistoric precision. It was ingenuous. His measurements lacked the rigidity of the orchestrated Mozartian symphonies. They were closer to the improvisations of New Orleans jazz.

Stukeley's suggestion that Stonehenge's diameter was 60 cubits or 104'(31.7 m) erred by 7'from Petrie's (1880, 23) figure of 97'4" ± 0.7" (29.7 m). It is an irony that Stukeley scorned Wood's far better estimate of 97'(29.6 m) (1747, 23), denouncing it in a letter of 3 August 1769 as a 'tedious parade of feet, inches, halfs and quarters' (Lukis, III, 275). In 1666 John Aubrey (1980, 75) was even closer to the truth with 36 yards $\frac{1}{2}'$, 97'6" (29.7 m). John Arbuthnot (Note 30); John Greaves (Note 31).

Rowldrich: the Rollright Stones circle, Oxfordshire, which Stukeley casually visited in 1710, returning with much more interest in 1724.

20 *Camp de Mart*: the Campus Martius, a spacious area at the west of Rome behind the Capitoline Hill in a bend of the River Tiber.

21 'Henges': these were natural stacks of weathered stones in Yorkshire and the Peak District enthusiastically interpreted as 'Druidical Rocking Stones'. (*Archaeologia 7*, 1785, 175–7; *ibid 8*, 1787, 209–17).

22 Giants' Dance, '*Chorea Gigantum*': see Thorpe, 1969, 172–3*.

23 Bell barrow nearest Stonehenge: Amesbury 11, SU 124 421.

24 Aurelius Ambrosius, the British war-leader whose actions were recorded in an early sixth-century chronicle by the monk, Gildas*: 'His' barrow was the plain bowl, 'King Barrow',

Amesbury 23, at SU 135 413 on Coneybury Hill (Grinsell, 1957, 150). Well to its west were the barrow cemeteries of Lake, Normanton and Wilsford.

25 John Webb (1611–72). Married the niece of Inigo Jones and was the author of *A Vindication of Stone-Heng Restored*, 1665, 2nd edition, 1725, a defence of Jones's contention that the Romans had built Stonehenge.

26 Aelius Donatus: fourth-century AD Roman grammarian. A tutor of St Jerome. His two books of Latin grammar were used throughout the Middle Ages. They were called 'Donats'.

27 Festus: Sextus Pompeius Festus, second-century AD Roman grammarian. Ennius: Quintus Ennius, late third-century BC Roman playwright.

28 '*Aruspicer*': haruspicer, a soothsayer, diviner.

29 Diameter of Stonehenge. Stukeley's 60 Celtic cubits (104 feet; 31.7 m) was an overestimate of 7 feet, a typical example of Stukeley's fitting the distance to conform with his lineal theories.

30 John Greaves (1602–52), mathematician and astronomer. Visited Egypt in 1638–9 and measured the Great Pyramid of Khufu [Cheops]. Richard Cumberland (1631–1718), Bishop of Peterborough. A friend of Samuel Pepys. In his *Sanchoniatho's Phoenician History*, published posthumously by his son-in-law in 1720, Cumberland attempted to prove that heathen gods had once been mortal men.

31 John Arbuthnot (1667–1735),

Scottish physician and writer, friend of Jonathan Swift. In a series of published satires against the Duke of Marlborough, Arbuthnot invented the character of John Bull.

32 In his *Pyramidographia* of 1646, Greaves (Note 31) recorded the Great Pyramid's base as 752′(229.2 m), only 3′from the original 440 Egyptian Cubits, a length of 755′(230.1 m). Stukeley may have omitted the figure as it was not the claimed 400 of his hypothetical Druids' Cubits but 433.9. (Berriman, 72)*.

33 The 'Cell': The internal horseshoe-shaped setting of five lintelled trilithons, 'three stones, inside the sarsen circle of Stonehenge.'

34 'Two great stones': the two pillars of the Great Trilithon, sarsens 55 and 56, of which 55 is fallen and now lies on a 'pyramid', stone 67, of the bluestone horseshoe. The numbering of the stones follows Petrie's system of 1880. From outside to centre it extends clockwise from the north-eastern axis and is 1 to 30 for the outer rings of sarsens; 31 to 49 for the surviving sixty pillars of the bluestone circle; 51 to 60 for the ten uprights of the five trilithons; 61 to 72 for the remaining nine standing stones of the 19-stone bluestone horseshoe. 80 is the Altar Stone; 91 to 96 the outlying stones; 91 to 94 the Four Stations; 95 the Slaughter Stone; 96 the Heel Stone. The lintels 'are all numbered 100 more than their higher numbered supporter' so that the heavy lintel at the entrance on

top of sarsens 1 and 30 became number 130.

35 A 'palm' measured $3\frac{1}{2}''$.

36 Abraham Sturgis, 'an architect'. Twenty years later John Wood (1747, 60) derided such a ludicrous aggrandisement of Stukeley's labourer. Sturges was, Wood noted, 'a jobing Bricklayer and Mason' from nearby Amesbury.

37 Constantius: the Roman emperor, Constantine the Great, c. AD 274–337.

38 Stukeley was referring to the irregular ring of some sixty bluestones between the sarsen circle and the inner trilithons.

39 The other bluestones were not a circle but a horseshoe of nineteen well-shaped uprights inside the trilithon horseshoe.

40 Hermogenes: early second-century BC architect from Asia Minor who preferred the Ionic style to the Doric. His *pseudo dipteros* was a false double portico to enhance an entrance.

41 These previously unnoticed observations are Stukeley at his best. Over the entrance to Stonehenge the lintel, stone 130, was heavier and more impressive than the others. The sarsens of the circle were twice as wide as the gaps between them, 7′against $3\frac{1}{2}'$. (Burl, 1987, 181–2).

42 The 'editor' of *Stonehenge Restored*, 1655, was Inigo Jones. His plan of four 'equilateral triangles' can be seen on his pages 59–60, Plan 2. 'The Groundplot of the work as when first built in a greater form with the four equilaterall trian-

gles making the *Scheame*, by which the whole work was composed'.

43 Pausanius, c. AD 130: a Greek traveller and geographer, author of the *Description of Greece, I–X*, a history and topography of famous cities and their cults. Book I, 'Attica & Megara'.

44 Outer circle, sarsens 1–30; pyramidal circle, bluestone ring, now stones 31–49.

45 David Loggan (1635–1700?), artist and engraver who published lavishly illustrated books of Oxford and Cambridge. He also made two well-known engravings of Stonehenge.

46 Female menstrual cycle.

47 Jones, 1655, 62–4.

48 'Pyramidal stones': the bluestone circle (Note 44).

49 A mistaken bluestone of the horseshoe. The pieces were three broken fragments of trilithon 59–60's lintel, 160a, b and c.

50 K. K: the two bluestone 49 and 31 across the north-east gap of the circle.

51 Helena: British-born wife of emperor Constantius Chlorus. She supposedly founded basilicas in the Holy Land at the Mount of Olives and at Bethlehem.

52 Godmandham: Goodmanham, SE 88. 42, near Market Weighton. A church on the site of a pagan temple burnt down in the year when Edwin of Northumbria was converted to Christianity by Paulinus in AD 627.

53 Arnobius: third-century AD Roman philosopher who converted to Christianity.

54 Macrobius: c. AD 400, wrote *Saturnalia I–VI*, describing witty conversations at a literary banquet.

55 Page 38. Stukeley's arithmetic. His 'precise' cubit is a moveable feast, varying from 18.6″, 19″ and 20.5″ (47.2, 48.3, 52.1 cm). As he was to remark about the ditch at Avebury, 'This is done with a sufficient, tho' not mathematical exactness. They were not careful in this great measure, where preciseness would have no effect' (1743, 19–20)*. Stukeley claimed he was numerate. 'Whilst I was at university I acquir'd a very good foundation in the mathematics & I own it is very bewitching' (Bodleian MS Eng. misc. c. 323, 266).

56 Theodosius the Great, c. AD 346–95, Roman emperor at Constantinople. Heliopolis was the 'City of the Sun', Syria.

57 Parvaim: an unknown region, perhaps the semi-mythical Ophir. 'And he garnished the house with precious stones for beauty, and the gold was gold from Parvaim', (*Chronicles II*, 3, 6).

58 Vitruvius Pollio, first-century BC architect, author of *De Architectura, I–X*. Book IV, 'Temples and the orders of architecture'.

59 Stukeley was correct. The trilithons do rise in height towards the south-west.

60 Stone 55 of the Great Trilithon fell inwards, its lintel smashing into bluestone 67 and dropping onto the Altar Stone. Stone 55 broke as it crashed onto the other end of the Altar Stone.

Stone 56 remaining standing but leaning inwards.

61 Buckingham dug at the centre of Stonehenge in 1620 (Aubrey, 1980, 93; Webb, 1725, 23).

62 Trilithon 57–58 was perfect. Trilithon 59–60 collapsed and its lintel broke into three pieces, 160a, b, and c.

63 Geologically Stukeley erred. The Altar Stone is not marble but sandstone.

64 Lintel 154 of trilithon 53–54 that stands in the southern arc of Stonehenge.

65 The bluestone horseshoe, originally of nineteen shaped stones, now ruinous. The eastern side has gone. Only nine others now stand, Petrie's numbers 61, 62, 63, 64, 65, 68, 69, 70.

66 Marius Servius Honoratus, early fifth-century AD grammarian, and commentator on Virgil's *Georgics*. His Latin grammar was intended for schools. The first version, *Servian*, was lengthened and became the *Servius auctus*.

67 Clemens: St. Clement of Alexandria, c. AD 150–215.

68 Diodorus Siculus, a first-century BC uncritical historian who wrote *Biblioteca historica*, 'Historical Library', in forty books, from antiquity to Caesar's Gallic Wars, 58 BC.

69 Stonehenge unknown before Henry VIII? Early twelfth-century Henry of Huntingdon (Note 7). Mid-twelfth-century Geoffrey of Monmouth claimed Merlin brought the sarsens from Ireland*.

70 Edward Stillingfleet, 1635–99, Bishop of Worcester, theologian of comparative religions. He compiled a detailed enquiry into the roots of religion (Note 92).

71 Apollodorus of Athens, second-century BC Greek historian. Ammianus Marcellinus, c. AD 330–95, wrote a history of Rome.

72 Thomas Cooper, Elizabethan author of a popular history and late night compiler of a Latin dictionary. His sleepless wife threw half of it onto the fire (Aubrey, 1949, 71).

73 Entrances: Stukeley did not notice the narrow gap at the exact south. There may also have been a blocked entrance at the north-west (Cleal et al, 110–11).

74 Earthwork diameter of Stonehenge, 400′(121.9 m)? Ditch to ditch, 374′6″ ± 10″ (114.2 ± 0.2 m), (Petrie, 22).

75 The Slaughter Stone, stone 95, prostrate at the north-east entrance of Stonehenge, measures 21′6″ × 6′9″ × 2′9″ (6.6 m) (Stone, 1924, 118)*.

76 The outlying Heel Stone, stone 96, a rough, leaning sarsen, measures 16′(4.9 m) × 9′× 6′10″ (Stone, 128, Plate 34)*.

77 'E'. According to Jones (1655, 57) around 1620 the Slaughter Stone was 20′ high (6.1 m), 7′wide and 3′thick. Some forty years later it had fallen but its partner, E, still stood (Aubrey, 1980, 76). By Stukeley's time it had gone.

78 Width of bank, mid-ditch to mid-ditch, 68′(20.7 m), much shorter than '75 Celtic feet' (22.9 m).

79 The two stones: Station Stone 91 at ENE, 'to the east', leaning then, now fallen; Station Stone

93, now a stump, is at the WNW not 'north-west'.

80 The avenue stones were unmentioned by Stukeley in his *Stonehenge*, 1740. In a letter of 20 May 1740, Gale rebuked Stukeley for the omission (Lukis, III, 268). In 1993 the combined results of geo-physical and electromagnetic testing afforded the probability that stones had once stood along the bank, spaced 93′6″ apart (28.5 m) (Castleden, 1993, 131–2).

81 Stukeley's computations were good considering the ruins that he measured. In order, the number of stones were: Altar Stone (1); lintels of the trilithons (5); the trilithon uprights (10); 'pyramidal' bluestone horseshoe, 19 rather than 20 (Atkinson, 1979, 42; Cleal et al, 29); sarsen circle stones (30); circle lintels (3); bluestone circle 60 ± 1 rather than 40 (Atkinson, 1979, 49; Cleal et al, 29); 'circle' of the Station Stones, 4 rather than 2. Probable total 140 + 21 = 161.

82 Ambrosius Theodosius Macrobius (Note 54).

83 *Basso releivos*: 'basso relievo', high relief elevation of a surface design.

84 *Thuribulum*, a vessel in which incense had burned, discovered by Inigo Jones. 'When I caused the foundations of the stones to be searched, my self found, and yet have by me to shew the cover of a *Thuribulum* or some like vase' (Jones, 1655, 76).

85 Faustina: probably the wife of Antoninus Pius, AD 86–168, in whose reign the Antonine Wall was built across Scotland. Coins were struck in her honour.

'SA', 'Senatus et Antoninus', the Senate and the emperor of Rome.

86 '*main amber*': nothing to do with Ambrosius. It was a 'shaking' or rocking stone near Penzance a 'famous stone, *Main-Amber*, which, being a great Rock, advanced on some other of meaner size with so equall a counterpeize, a man may stir with the push of his finger' (Camden, 1637, 188; Stukeley, 1740, 49–51).

87 '*Lapis unctus betylus*': an oily meteoric stone.

88 Amesbury: desperate place-name analysis by Stukeley. Around AD 880 the first recorded name was *Ambresbyrig*. 'Byrig' (Gover et al, 358–9)*, or fortified place, referring to the nearby Iron Age hillfort of Vespasian's Camp (Note 10). 'Ambre' is probably a folk-memory of Aurelius Ambrosius (Note 18).

89 Lead and tin tablet: 'Had it been preserved, somewhat happily might have been discovered as concerning *Stonehenge* which now lies obscured' (Camden, *Britain*, 1637, 254). The tablet was probably a *defixiones*, a curse-tablet on imperishable lead intended to harm an offender (Burl, 1987, 221).

90 Samuel Bochart (1559–1667), French theologian born in Rouen, a famous orientalist and biblical scholar.

91 Pliny: 'It is unanimously agreed that the Ionians were the first of all to use letters'.

92 Stillingfleet (Note 70). In his *Origines Britannicae*, 1685, he com-

pared Greek, Phoenician, Chaldean, Egyptian and Hebraic myths. 'Markolis' was a Hebraic custom of worshipping an idol by throwing stones at its temple. The Roman god, Mercurius, was associated both with the name and the practice. Johann Buxtorf, 1564–1629, student of Hebrew religion. Pausanius (Note 43): the *Achaea* was the seventh of the ten books in his *History of Greece*.

93 Pausanius: Note 43.

94 A roofed Stonehenge. Two centuries after Stukeley an article, 'The use of wood in megalithic structures' by Vayson de Pradenne, 1957, 87–92*, suggested that the ring had been covered.

95 Homer, *Iliad, I*, 448–75. For a modern translation of the lines see: E. V. Rieu, P. Jones and D. C. H. Rieu, 6–17.

96 *Iliad, II*, 426–7. (Note 95, p. 32).

97 Discovery of the avenue. In 1666 John Aubrey, 1980, 97, referring to the outlying Heel Stone, observed that it stood 'in the Walke or Avenue' of which no stones remained. Stukeley was the first to recognise the indistinct banks and ditches. He also saw stones along it but later denied their existence (Note 80).

98 The '7 barrows' were the New King round barrows (Note 12) lying N–S just south of the eastern extension of the avenue. Several decades after Stukeley they were planted with Scots firs.

99 The three stretches of the avenue: (i) Laid out around 2200 BC, 1770 ± 70 BC, Cleal et al,

526, it led north-eastwards from Stonehenge for about 600 yards (550 m), then (ii) turned ESE for half a mile up to the northern-most of the New King barrows. There it may have bent (iii) sharply to the SSE towards the River Avon $\frac{3}{4}$ mile away. Perhaps started as late as c. 1500 BC, 1070 ± 180 BC, only its eastern bank was finished: (G. Smith, 1973, 42–56).* The dating of this 'third' stretch has been questioned (Cleal et al, 323–7).

100 No stones. This was written on a later page, 72, that was added to the manuscript. For Stukeley's original belief in stones, see (Note 80).

101 *Ippodrom*, 'horse-race'. This was the Stonehenge Cursus $\frac{1}{2}$ mile north of Stonehenge, $1\frac{3}{4}$ miles long, 120 yards (110 m) wide rectangular enclosure with curved ends. It was oriented WSW–ESE, 267°–87°. It has no obvious solar or lunar alignment.

102 '5 old barrows', in fact eight or nine bowl and bell round barrows, the Old King group centred on SU 137 429.

103 Virgil, *Georgics III*, 103.

104 Diodorus Siculus (Note 68). Panchea was a Arabian island famous for its perfumes.

105 236' long (71.9 m) *meta*: In Rome a *meta* was a pillar as a turning point at either end of a race-track.

106 Barrows. Stukeley decided that the plain bowl and ditched bell round barrows were simply 'barrows'. The dainty discs with circular ditch and bank around a tiny round mound at their very centre were 'Druid

barrows'. Long barrows were 'Arch-druid' burial-places. The 'prodigious' sight of barrows towards Shrewton was the Winterbourne Stoke group $1\frac{1}{2}$ miles west of Stonehenge, SU 101 417, a mixture of bells, bowls, discs, saucers and a long barrow: (Grinsell, 1978, 18).

107 Viorna: *viburnum*, Latin, 'wayfaring tree', attractive, small evergreens.

108 Paedian: Q. Asconius Pedianus, historian, early first-century AD, reported many of Cicero's speeches including those against Mark Antony and Catiline. Livy (Titus Livius), 59 BC–AD 17, wrote a long history of Rome in 142 books of which only thirty-five survive: I–X, XXI–XXX and XXXI–XLV. The work was entitled *Decades* as it was arranged in groups of ten books. Pliny the Elder, AD 23–79, wrote widely but only the thirty-seven books of his *Historia Naturalis* survive.

109 Stukeley was mistaken. His 'western' branch of the avenue was the remains of a medieval trackway.

110 Pausanius (Note 43). The 'Phoenix' occurs in the section of his *Description of Greece* concerned with remains of antiquity and mythology.

111 Thomas Hayward was the owner of Stonehenge.

112 The leaning stone was Trilithon 56. In 1660 it tilted at an angle of 75°, 15° from the perpendicular; in 1720 at 70°; in 1870 dangerously at 66°. It was finally straightened and set in concrete in 1901 by Gowland*.

113 Cizycus. Stukeley muddled two legends. In the *Argonautica Orphica*, the story of Jason and the Golden Fleece, reputedly written by Orpheus, Jason sailing to the Black Sea passed through the narrow Propontis where he was welcomed by Cizycus (Kyzikos), the ruler. On the argonauts' departure they were driven back by storms, were mistaken for pirates and in the fighting Jason killed Cizycus. Great funeral games were held. Another version stated that Cizycus had killed a lion of the goddess, Rhea. In revenge she made Hercules, one of the argonauts, kill Cizycus (Apollonius of Rhodes *Jason and the Golden Fleece, Book I*). (Graves, *I*, 82, 280; *II*, 149, 223–7)*.

114 Excavations at Stonehenge. For references, see: Grinsell, 1957. Pembroke's twin bell-barrow south of Stonehenge was Wilsford South 15W, SU 120 412.

115 Patroclus. Stukeley was mistaken. No horses raced around the hero's pyre. They were sacrificed: Homer, *Iliad I, XVIII, XIX*. Pallas was killed fighting for Aeneas: Virgil, *Aeneid XI*.

116 Adjoining barrow: twin-bell Amesbury 44E. SU 119 427. The blue beads were faience.

117 On Stukeley's pages 84, 86 and 97 he refers to entries in the *Philosophical Transactions* concerning burials lying north–south, cremations and golden urns. The particular volumes, their date and the relevant pages are only vaguely identified. A diligent search by the librarian of the Society of Antiquaries of London through the *Transactions*

held by the Royal Astronomical Society led to his conclusion that Stukeley's 'references . . . are wholly inaccurate, and there is no index to the early volumes which is of any use'. It is a frustration shared by the present writer having elsewhere futilely inspected the *Transactions* himself. However interesting Stukeley's comments are his sources remain elusive.

118 The next barrow: twin-bell Amesbury 44W, SU 119 427. As was customary in Wessex, men were buried with their heads towards the north.

119 Georg Keysler, (1689–1743), antiquarian, who pointed out the similarity of European and British pre-Roman tombs in his *Antiquitates Selectae Septentrionales et Celticae*, Hanover, 1720.

120 Pomponius Mela, first-century AD Roman geographer, author *of De Situ Orbis, I–III*, 'The World's Places'.

121 Valerius Maximus, first-century AD, who wrote *Facta et Dicta Memorabilia, I–IX*, 'Memorable Deeds and Sayings'.

122 Diodorus (Note 68) book V, *Europe*. Heraclitus, (c. 540–480 BC), Greek philosopher. Servius (Note 66).

123 A small barrow: a bowl, one of Amesbury 1, 2, or 3. SU 115 418.

124 A barrow near Bush Barrow is the splendid bell, Amesbury 15, SU 115 416.

125 Revd Edward Duke of Lake House, antiquarian, (1779–1852), who in one of the Lake barrows found some perplexingly decorated bone tablets similar to others in Yorkshire*.

126 'Divine ghosts or good spirits'. William Baxter, (1650–1723), whose *Horace* was published in 1701.

127 The source is misquoted and does not appear in Cicero's *Philippics IX* or *XI*. Nor can a reference to a burial with violated bones and ashes be found in the twelve books of Quintilian's *Institutio oratoria*, c. AD 35.

128 Druid's barrow: a disc, Wilsford South 4, SU 115 412.

129 Three barrows: (i) a long barrow, Wilsford South 13, SU 118 413, lying SW–NE, only 65′long (19.8 m); (ii) Druid's barrow, a disc, Wilsford South 14, SU 119 412 by Lord Pembroke's; (iii) twin-bell, Wilsford South 16, SU 120 412.

130 'Three little barrows': one of the small bowls, Amesbury 20–22, SU 129 418.

131 Fifth barrow: Amesbury 28, a bowl of the New King group, SU 134 216.

132 'Old flat barrow' with bluestone chippings: Amesbury 4 bowl, SU 118 421.

133 'Ambrosius Barrow': King Barrow, Amesbury 23 (Note 24/5). The 'poleaxe' was a Middle Bronze Age halberd weighing about 22 lbs (10 kg).

134 Edward Lhuyd, (1660–1709). Welsh antiquarian, a contemporary of John Aubrey. His invaluable notes of fieldwork in Britain, Ireland and Brittany were unpublished except for a long letter from Oxford of 13 September 1696 which was published in Camden's *Britannia*, 1697, 583ff. Stukeley copied from the manuscripts copiously and sometimes inaccurately.

135 'A great barrow': Waldershare Park, Kent, TR 29. 48., just NNW of Dover. The barrow may have been dug by Cromwell Mortimer, an 'impertinent, assuming, empyric physician' and member of the revived Royal Society. (Marsden, 1999, 13)*.

136 Pausanius, (Notes 43, 110). The reference is to Book IV of his *Elis*, a *Description of Greece*.

137 Tacitus, *Germania XXVII*, 2. *sepulchrum caespes erigit . . .* : 'In burial there is no ostentation: the single observance is to burn the bodies of their notables with special kinds of wood. They build a pyre but do not load it with palls or spices; to each man his armour: to the fire of some his horse is added. The tomb is a mound of turf: The difficult and tedious tribute of a monument they reject as too heavy on the dead'.

138 Snorro: Snorre Sturlason, (1179–1241), Icelandic historian, author of *Heimskringla*, 'Saga of the Norwegian Kings', Book XXII, Alexander I – Alexander V.

139 Servius Honoratus, (Note 66) an early fifth-century AD unreliable commentator on Virgil: 'That clown . . . Servius', (Levi, 1998, 33, 124)*.

140 Philostratus, late second-century AD Greek writer. Strabo, late first-century BC author of *Geography, Book XVII*, 'Egypt and Africa'.

141 'Bowing Stone', Stukeley's term for the leaning Heel Stone, no. 96. 'Flat Stone', the Slaughter Stone, no. 95.

142 Florus Quintus Septimius Tertullianus, (AD 160–225), Latin theologian, author of *Apology for the Christians*. Servius (Note 66).

143 Caesar, *Gallic War, VI, xviv*; Tacitus, *Germania, XXVII*.

144 'Monumental stones', the megalithic tombs known as *hunebedden* at Drenthe, Holland (Service & Bradbery)*. Johann Georg Keysler (1689–1743), author of *Antiquitates Selectae Septentrionales et Celticae*, 1740.

145 'Necham': Alexander Neckham, (1157–1217), Abbot of Cirencester. He wrote extensively about science, grammar, Latin poetry, theology and Aristotle.

146 Apollonius of Rhodes, third-century BC author of the *Argonautica, I*, the epic poem of Jason and the argonauts in search of the Golden Fleece.

147 'Goodmansfield': probably Godmanham near Great Walsingham, Norfolk, where a round barrow was excavated in the seventeenth-century (Browne, II)*.

148 Keysler (Note 144). *Drouven* is a farmland near Drenthe in Holland with many prehistoric long mounds known as *hunebedden*, 'giants' beds'.

149 Measurements. As already noted the distances quoted in Druids' Cubits are very approximate. The measurements were painstakingly taken but the records are frequently more convenient to Stukeley's thesis than lineally accurate.

150 '*pamplyia obelisc*': an obelisk in Pamphylia, a province in Asia Minor.

151 Lucan: Marcus Annaeus Lucanus (AD 39–65), historian,

author of *De Bello Civile*.
Kircher: Athanasius Kircher,
(1602–80), Jesuit scholar.

152 'Porta thausti': the entrance to the
famous temple of Hercules on
Thasos, an island in Thrace,
'rich in gold and silver mines,
marble and wine'.

153 Wittekind, a Saxon leader who
fought Charlemagne and was
killed in AD 807 (*De Gesta
Saxonni*).

154 Eusebius, (c. AD 260–339),
Bishop of Caesarea, author of
Ecclesiastical History, I–X.

155 'bembin table': The Bembine
Tablet of bronze and silver
engraved with hieroglyphics and
with the goddess, Isis, at its
centre. It was thought to be the
key to ancient alphabets. It
vanished during the sack of
Rome in AD 1527.

156 Porphryry or Porphyrios, 'the
purple one', (c. AD 234–c. 305),
an anti-Christian philosopher
and Tyrian scholar, 'the great
enemy the Christian religion
ever had'. His books were
publicly burnt in AD 448.
The quotation beginning,
'Egyptioru aute diori' . . . is from
his *Enneads*. Stukeley used it to
support his belief that 'this oval
figure of Stonehenge thus
encompassed by circles' was a
recreation of the sacred egg of
the world, 'the *ova Mundus*', the
eternal shape of the gods. He
quoted two imperfectly-known
gods. Their names were mis-
spelled, probably through an
inability accurately to decipher
Egyptian hieroglyphics.
They were mentioned by
Porphyrys, 'Ptha graeci vulcanuu
appellant', actually *Ptah*, a god of

Memphis and the Greek Vulcan,
a creator god; and *Emepli*, the
god *Amun* of Thebes, 'nemini
conspicuu', 'the invisible one'.
According to Stukeley, druids
used the shapes assumed by
these deities to design the circle
and 'ovals' of Stonehenge. He
did the same three years in his
Abury of 1743.

157 Woad: Pliny, *Natural History
XXII, ii*.

158 Dionysius Periegetes, second-
century geographer who wrote
the *Description of the World*.

159 The list of bearings of monuments to and from Stonehenge
is a tribute to Stukeley's commit-
ment to fieldwork. Regrettably
his theodolite was probably
fitted with a faulty magnetic
compass whose accuracy seems
to have been in error by 1°30″ ±
3°, perhaps disturbed by the
jogging as it was taken by horse-
back from site to site (Atkinson,
1985). As a result the 'entrance
of Stonehenge' was not '4
degrees East from the true
Northeast', that is, 4° south-east
of 45°, 49°. The true bearing
was 49°57′± 3′(Thom et al, 1974,
81). In consequence Stukeley's
'bearings' erred by up to −4° to
the east of Stonehenge, and +4°
to its west. As examples, the
circle did not lie 32° but 36° to
the NNE of Bush Barrow, and
the ring was not $58\frac{1}{2}°$ [238°30′]
but 61° [241°] to the WSW of
the centre of the New King
barrow group.

160 The burial of Drusus: Tacitus,
Annals II, vii. Suetonius, Graves,
R.*

161 'Winkind de Woord': Wynken
de Worde, (d. 1534?), real name

Jan van Wynken, pupil of William Caxton. He was the first printer in England to use italics. Stukeley may have been referring to his edition of Malory's *Morte d'Arthur* of 1493 in which Merlin is a seminal figure.

162 'Mr. Marten': Martin Martin (d. 1719), *A Description of the Western Islands of Scotland*, 1703. The book so interested Samuel Johnson that it enticed him to visit the Hebrides.

163 The ignorance of the Gauls about Britain: Caesar, *The Gallic War, IV, xx.*

164 This is Stukeley's list of page references in his manuscript.

165 Mr. Jay: Robert Gay, rector of Nettlecombe, Somerset, from 1631 to 1672, author of a fanciful and farcical book about Stonehenge. See the Bibliography.

166 Materials in the open air: Stukeley was perceptive and correct. Builders of stone circles built them where stones lay freely in the countryside. They did not quarry. In inhabited regions where there was no stone available sites such as causewayed enclosures and henges were constructed of earth. There were also rings of posts in wooded areas.

167 For current thinking about prehistoric building methods, see: Atkinson, 1979, 102–41; Burl, 1987, 130–7, 172–85; J. Richards & M. Whitby, 'The engineering of Stonehenge', in: Cunliffe & Renfrew, 1997, 231–56*.

168 Carlo Fontana, (c. 1638–1714), a Swiss papal architect in Rome.

REFERENCES *

Ashe, G., *A Guidebook to Arthurian Britain*, Longman, London, 1980, 5–6.

Berriman, A. E., *Historical Metrology*, Dent, London, 1953, 72.

Browne, Sir Thomas, intro, C. H. Herford, 'Hydriotaphia, or Urn Burial', in *'The 'Religio Medici and other Writings'*, J. M. Dent, London, 1658, 102.

Burl, A. 2002, see: Duke, E.

Cunliffe, B. & Renfrew, C., eds. *Science and Stonehenge*, British Academy, Oxford, 1997, 231–56.

Duke, Revd E., *The Druidical Temples of the County of Wilts.*, John Russell Smith, London, 1846; the carved tablets, ibid, *VCH Wilts, I*, 1, 1957, 211; A. Burl, *Prehistoric Avebury*, 2002, 235–7.

Forester, T., trans. & ed., *The Chronicle of Henry of Huntingdon*, Llanerch Press, Felinfach, 1991, 7.

Geoffrey of Monmouth, *Historia Regum Britanniae* ('The History of the Kings of Britain'), *Part VI*, 172–3, trans. L. Thorpe, Folio Society, London, 1969.

Gildas, *De Excidio et Conquestu Britanniae*, 'The Ruin of Britain and Other Works', trans & ed., M. Winterbottom, Phillimore, Chichester, 1978.

Gowland, W. 'Recent excavations at Stonehenge', *Wiltshire Archaeological & Natural History Magazine 33 (99)*, 1903, 1–620.

Gover, J. E. B., Mawer, A., & Stenton, F. M., *The Place-Names of Wiltshire*, Cambridge University Press, 1970.

Graves, R. *The Greek Myths, I, II*, Penguin, Harmondsworth, 1955, *I*, 82, 280; *II*, 149, 223–7.

——Suetonius, *The Twelve Caesars. Gaius Suetonius Tranquillus*, trans. R. Graves, Penguin, Harmondsworth, 1957, Claudius *I*, 181–207.

Lever, T., *The Herberts of Wilton*, John Murray, London, 1967, *42*, 48–9.

Levi, P., *Virgil. His Life and Times*, St. Martin's Press, New York, 1998, *33*, 124.

Long, W., *Stonehenge and Its Barrows*, Devizes, 1876, 187.

Marsden, B., *The Early Barrow Diggers*, Tempus, Stroud, 1999, *13*.

Piggott, S., 'Stukeley, Avebury and the Druids', *Antiquity IX*, 1935, 22–32.

Pradenne, Vayson de, 'The use of wood in megalithic structures', *Antiquity XI*, 1937, 87–92.

Rieu, E. V., Jones, P. and Rieu, D. C. H., *Homer. The Odyssey*, Penguin, London, 2003, 16–17.

Service, A. & Bradbery, J., *The Standing Stones of Europe*, J. M. Dent, London, 1993, 'Holland, *Drenthe*, 150–8.

Smith, G., 'Excavation of the Stonehenge avenue at West Amesbury, Wiltshire, *WAM 68*, 1973, 42–56.

Stone, H., *The Stones of Stonehenge*, Robert Scott, London, 1924.

References

Stukeley, W., *Abury, a Temple of the British Druids, with some Others Described*, Innys, Manby, Dod, & Brindley, London, 1743.

Thorpe, L., *Geoffrey of Monmouth. 'The History of the Kings of Britain*, Folio Society, London, 1969, 172–3.

BIBLIOGRAPHY

(A. Classical)

Ammianus Marcellinus, *History, III*, trans. J. C. Rolfe, Heinemann, London, 1964, 52–3.

Caesar, *The Gallic War*, trans. H. J. Edwards, Heinemann, London, 1979.

Claudian, *Poems*, (Vol. II), trans. D. E. Eichholz, Heinemann, London, 1972, 224–5.

Diodorus Siculus, *The Library of History, II*, (Vol. 1), trans. C. H. Oldfather, Heinemann, London, 1979.

—— *IX–XII*, (Vol. IV), trans. C. H. Oldfather, Heinemann, London, 1946.

Livy, History of Rome, *XXVII*, trans. F. G. Moore, Heinemann, London, 1971.

Lucan, *Pharsalia, The Civil War*, Trans. J. D. Duff, Heinemann, London, 1969.

Ovid, *Metamorphoses X*, (Vol. 2), trans. F. J. Miller, Heinemann, London, 1916, 76–7.

—— *XIII*, (Vol. 2), trans. F. J. Miller, Heinemann, London, 1916, 144–5.

Pliny the Elder, *Natural History VII* (Vol. 2), trans. H. Rackham, Heinemann, London, 1942, 646–7.

—— *XII–XVI*, (Vol. 1), trans. H. Rackham, Heinemann, London, 1958, 284–5.

—— *XXII*, (Vol. 2) trans. W. H. S. Jones, Heinemann, London, 1969, 294–5.

—— *XXXVI*, (Vol. 10), trans. D. E. Eichholz, Heinemann, London, 1971, 50–1.

Propertius, *Elegies*, trans. G. P. Goold, Harvard, Cambridge, Mass. and London, 1990, 202–3.

Quintillian, (Vol. VII), trans. D. A. Russell, Harvard, Cambridge, Mass. and London, 2001, 226 *The Orator's Education, VI–VIII–*7.

Tacitus, *Annals II*, (Vol. V), trans. J. Jackson, Heinemann, London, 1969.

Tertullian, *Apology. De Speculatis*, trans. T. R. Glover, Heinemann, London, 1966.

Virgil, *Eclogues, Georgics, Aeneid I–VI*, trans. H. R. Fairclough & G. P. Goold, Harvard, Cambridge, Mass. and London, 1999: *Aeneid, II*, 350–1: VI, 522–3.

—— *ibid, Georgics*, 252–3.

(B. Post-Classical)

Atkinson, R. J. C. (1979) *Stonehenge. Archaeology and Interpretation*, 2nd edition, Penguin, Harmondsworth.

—— (1985) 'William Stukeley and the Stonehenge sunrise', *Journal for the History of Astronomy*, S61–2.

Aubrey, J., (1949) *Aubrey's 'Brief Lives'*, ed. O. L. Dick, Secker & Warburg, London.

Bibliography

——(1980) *Monumenta Britannica, I*, (1665–97). Dorset Publishing, Milborne Port.

——(1982) *Monumenta Britannica, II*, (1665–97). Dorset Publishing, Milborne Port.

Burl, A., (1987) *The Stonehenge People*, J. M. Dent, London.

——(1999) *Great Stone Circles. Fables, Fictions Facts*, Yale University Press, New Haven and London.

——(2000) *The Stone Circles of Britain, Ireland and Brittany*, Yale University Press, New Haven and London.

Camden, W., (1637) *Britain, or a Chorographicall Description of the most flourishing Kingdoms, England, Scotland and Ireland*, Latham, London.

——(1695) *Britannia, Newly Translated into English: with Large Additions and Improvements*, ed. E. Gibson, A. Swalle, London.

Castleden, R., (1993) *The Making of Stonehenge*, Routledge, London.

Charleton, W., (1663) *Chorea Gigantum; or, The Most Famous Antiquity of Great-Britan, Vulgarly called Stone-heng, Standing on Salisbury Plain, Restored to the Danes*, Herringman, London.

Chippindale, C., (2004) *Stonehenge Complete*, Revised Edition, Thames & Hudson, London.

Cleal, M. J., Walker, K. E. & Montague, R., (1995) eds. *Stonehenge in its Landscape. Twentieth Century Excavations*, English Heritage, London.

Gay, Revd R., (c. 1666) *A Fool's Bolt soon shott at Stonage*, in Legg, 1986, 5–37.

Grinsell, L. V., (1957) 'Archaeological Gazetteer', in Pugh, R. B. & Crittall, E. eds. *A History of Wiltshire, I (1)*, Oxford University Press, Oxford, 21–279.

——(1978) *The Stonehenge Barrow Groups*, Salisbury & South Wiltshire Museum, Salisbury.

Hatchwell, R. & Burl, A., (1998) 'The Commonplace Book of William Stukeley', *Wiltshire Archaeological & Natural History Magazine, 91*, 65–75.

Haycock, D. B., (2002) *William Stukeley. Science, Religion and Archaeology in Eighteenth Century England*, Boydell Press, Woodbridge.

Jones, I., (1655) *The most notable Antiquity of Great Britain, vulgarly called Stone-Heng on Salisbury Plain*, Pakeman, London.

Legg, R., (1986) *Stonehenge Antiquaries*, Dorset Publishing Company, Milborne Port.

Lukis, Revd W. C., (1882) *The Family Memoirs of the Rev. William Stukeley, M. D. and the Antiquarian and other Correspondence of William Stukeley, Roger and Samuel Gale etc, I*, Surtees Society, Durham, London, Edinburgh.

——(1883) *Ibid, II*, Surtees Society, Durham, London, Edinburgh.

——(1887) *Ibid, III*, Surtees Society, Durham, London, Edinburgh.

McAdam, E. L. & Milne, G., (1982) *Johnson's Dictionary. A Modern Selection*, Book Club Associates, London.

Mortimer, N., (2003) *Stukeley Illustrated. William Stukeley's Rediscovery of Britain's Ancient Sites*, Green Magic Publishing, Sutton Mallet.

Petrie, W. M. F., (1880) *Stonehenge: Plans, Description, and Theories*, Stanford, London.

Piggott, S., (1935) 'Stukeley, Avebury and the Druids' *Antiquity, 9*, 22–32.

——(1950) *William Stukeley. An Eighteenth-Century Antiquary*, Thames & Hudson, London.

——(1951) 'William Camden and the *Britannia*', *Proceedings of the British Academy*, *37*, 199–217.

——(1971) Introduction, *Inigo Jones, STONE-HENG; Walter Charleton, CHOREA GIGANTUM, John Webb, A VINDICATION, London, 1725*, Gregg International, London.

——(1985) *William Stukeley. An Eighteenth-Century Antiquary*, 2nd edition, Thames & Hudson, London.

——(1989) *Ancient Britons and the Antiquarian Imagination, Ideas from the Restoration to the Regency*, Thames & Hudson, London.

Stukeley, W., (1722–4) 'THE HISTORY OF THE TEMPLES OF THE ANTIENT CELTS', I, II, Bodleian Library MS Eng. Misc. c. 323.

——(1740) *Stonehenge a Temple restored to the British Druids*, Innys & Manby, London.

——(1743) *Abury, a Temple of the British Druids, with Some Others, Described*, Innys, Manby, Dod & Brindley, London.

——(1776a) *Itinerarium Curiosum. Centuriae I*, (itineraries 1710–23) 2nd edition, Baker & Leigh, London.

——(1776b) *Itinerarium Curiosum, Centuria II*, (itinerary 1725), 2nd edition, Baker & Leigh, London.

Sweet, R., (2004) *Antiquaries. The Discovery of the Past in Eighteenth-Century Britain*, Hambledon and London, London.

Thom, A., A. S. & A. S., 'Stonehenge', *Journal of the History of Astronomy V*, 1974, 81.

Ucko P. J. et al, Hunter, M., Clark, A. J. & David, A., (1991) *Avebury Reconsidered. From the 1660s to the 1990s*, Unwin Hyman, London.

Webb, J., (1665) *A Vindication of Stone-Heng Restored: in which the Orders and Rules of Architecture observed by the Ancient Romans, are Discussed*, Conyers, Sprint, Lintot, Brown, Woodman & Lyon, London.

——(1725) *ibid*, 2nd edition.

Wood, J., (1747) *Choir Gaure, vulgarly called STONEHENGE, on Salisbury Plain . . .* , privately published, Oxford: Hitch, Birt, London: Leake and Bath: Collins, Salisbury.

INDEX

Bold numerals signify an important entry